ESSAYS ON SHAKESPEARE AND OTHER ELIZABETHANS

BY

TUCKER BROOKE

LATE STERLING PROFESSOR OF ENGLISH
YALE UNIVERSITY

NEW HAVEN

YALE UNIVERSITY PRESS

LONDON · GEOFFREY CUMBERLEGE · OXFORD UNIVERSITY PRESS

1948

THE OLIVER BATY CUNNINGHAM
MEMORIAL PUBLICATION FUND

The present volume is the twenty-fourth work published by the Yale University Press on the Oliver Baty Cunningham Memorial Publication Fund. This Foundation was established May 8, 1920, by a gift from Frank S. Cunningham, Esq., of Chicago, to Yale University, in memory of his son, Captain Oliver Baty Cunningham, 15th United States Field Artillery, who was born in Chicago, September 17, 1894, and was graduated from Yale College in the Class of 1917. As an undergraduate he was distinguished alike for high scholarship and for proved capacity in leadership among his fellows, as evidenced by his selection as Gordon Brown Prize Man from his class. He received his commission as Second Lieutenant, United States Field Artillery, at the First Officers' Training Camp at Fort Sheridan, and in December, 1917, was detailed abroad for service, receiving subsequently the Distinguished Service Medal. He was killed while on active duty near Thiaucourt, France, on September 17, 1918, the twenty-fourth anniversary of his birth.

PREFACE

GOOD wine needs no bush. Tucker Brooke was as eminent for the wit and charm of his writing as for the soundness of his scholarship. In the essays here reprinted he illustrated the true function of the scholar in relation to the community at large. They illuminate the subjects they discuss without the falsifications and distortions so characteristic of the half-learned popularizer, yet there is in them the unmistakable touch of his own personality. To praise them further would be a superfluity of which I would not be guilty.

The essays range in time from "King Lear on the Stage" in 1913 to "Shakespeare and the *Textus Receptus*" in 1945. Two of them, those on Spenser and Marlowe, have not previously been published and were written some time ago, probably in the early 'twenties. In spite of the fact that they were never passed for publication by the author I have thought it right to print them. They are among his best pieces of appreciative criticism, and certainly everyone will welcome the rescue of his praise of Marlowe, upon whom he lavished so much of his scholarly work. The essay on "Shakespeare Apart" has been reprinted from the original version in the *Yale Review* rather than from the enlarged text, entitled "The Personality of Shakespeare," which is still available in the *Shakespeare of Stratford* volume of the "Yale Shakespeare" series.

I am grateful to the *Yale Review*, the *Sewanee Review*, the *Huntington Library Quarterly*, the *Papers of the American Bibliographical Society, Studies in Philol-*

ogy, *Modern Language Notes*, **ELH**, and the Yale Romanic Studies for permission to reprint essays which appeared in their pages; also to the New York University Press for permission to reprint an essay from one of its publications. Specific acknowledgment of these sources is given in the Table of Original Appearances.

A number of Professor Brooke's former students have expressed a desire that a memorial volume might be published. I hope that this book, in which some of his own best work is gathered together, will be accepted by them as the most suitable tribute to the memory of a rare personality.

LEICESTER BRADNER

Brown University,
June 19, 1947.

TABLE OF ORIGINAL APPEARANCES

ESSAYS AND STUDIES IN HONOR OF CARLETON BROWN (New York University Press, 1940)
  "Shakespeare Remembers His Youth in Stratford"

ESSAYS IN HONOR OF ALBERT FEUILLERAT (Yale Romanic Studies, XXII, Yale University Press, 1943)
  "Willobie's *Avisa*"

THE YALE SHAKESPEARE, HENRY IV, PART I (Yale University Press, 1947)
  "Shakespeare and the *Textus Receptus*"

CONTENTS

SHAKESPEARE'S QUEEN

THE Mayor of London and his brethren of the corporation and forty of the chief citizens were commanded to be at the christening, on the tenth of September, 1533. "Upon which day"—so the old chronicler Holinshed informs us in one of his most picturesque accounts—"the Mayor, Sir Stephen Peacock, in a gown of crimson velvet with his collar of S's, and all the aldermen in scarlet with collars and chains, and all the council of the city with them, took their barge at one of the clock; and the citizens had another barge; and so rowed to Greenwich, where were many lords, knights, and gentlemen assembled. All the walls between the King's palace and the Friars' were hanged with arras, and all the way strewed with green rushes. The Friars' church was also hanged with rich arras: the font was of silver, and stood in the midst of the church three steps high, which was covered with a fine cloth; and divers gentlemen, *with aprons and towels around their necks*, gave attendance about it, that no filth should come to the font. . . . Between the choir and body of the church was a close place with a pan of fire, to make the Child ready in. When all these things were ordered, the Child was brought to the hall, and then every man set forward: first the citizens, two and two; then gentlemen, esquires, and chaplains; next after them the aldermen, and the Mayor alone; and next the King's Council; then the King's Chapel in copes; then barons, bishops, earls, the Earl of Essex bearing the covered basins, gilt; after him the Marquess of Exeter with a taper of virgin wax; next him the Marquess Dorset, bearing the salt; behind him the Lady Mary of Norfolk, bearing the chrism, which was very rich of pearl and stone.

"The old Duchess of Norfolk bare the Child in a mantle of purple velvet, with a long train furred with ermine. The Duke of Norfolk with his marshal's rod went on the right hand of the said Duchess, and the Duke of Suffolk on the left hand. . . . When the Child was come to the church door, the Bishop of London met it, with divers bishops and abbots mitred, and began the observances of the sacrament. The godfather was Lord Thomas [Cranmer], Archbishop of Canterbury; the godmothers were the old Duchess of Norfolk and old Marchioness of Dorset, widows: and the Child was named ELIZABETH. And after that all things were done at the church door, the Child was brought to the font and christened; and that done, Garter, chief king of arms, cried aloud: 'God of his infinite goodness send prosperous life and long to the high and mighty Princess of England, ELIZABETH!'

"And then the trumpets blew. Then the Child was brought up to the altar, and the gospel said over it. After that immediately the Archbishop of Canterbury confirmed it, the Marchioness of Exeter being godmother. . . . Then was brought in wafers, confects, and ipocras in such plenty that every man had as much as he would desire: then they set forward"—but somewhat less steadily, it may be, than before.

By this time, we learn with relief, the child had been restored to the seemlier precincts of the nursery, where she grew apace through all the stirring years, while her redoubtable father (of whom she was always inordinately proud) was sending to the beheading block the bulk of the distinguished company that had officiated at her baptismal orgy.

When death removed Henry the Eighth, Elizabeth had passed her thirteenth birthday. A gentleman of the court writes approvingly of her: "The Lady Elizabeth, which is at this time of the age of fourteen years, or thereabouts, is a very witty and gentle young lady." Gentle she did indeed show herself to be as long as her brother Edward ruled the land; the succeeding reign of her sister Mary called into play every atom of her superabundant wit. The reign of Edward the Sixth, which lasted from Elizabeth's fourteenth till her twentieth year, was the most charming part of her life. There was a tender affection between her and her young half-brother, both of whom lived like babes in the wood amid a flock of rascally, ambitious nobles. The boy king called her "his sweet sister Temperance"; she wrote him some of the nicest letters that a little princess ever composed, and she scribbled the name "Edward" lovingly over her exercise books.

The Tudors were a gifted lot; and Elizabeth had the best brain of them all, with a physique quite worthy of her father. "She was of admirable beauty," says Camden, "and well deserving a crown: of a modest gravity, excellent wit, royal soul, happy memory, and indefatigably given to the study of learning; insomuch as before she was seventeen years of age, she understood well the Latin, French, and Italian tongues, and had an indifferent knowledge of the Greek. Neither did she neglect music so far as it became a princess, being able to sing sweetly and play handsomely on the lute." Her hair was "inclining to pale yellow" (she was "whiter" than the red-haired Queen of Scots); her eyes were black, and her nose "somewhat rising in the midst." As Bacon tells us: "She was tall of stature, of comely limbs, and excellent feature in her countenance. Majesty sat under the veil of sweetness, and her health was sound and prosperous."

Elizabeth's proficiency in languages was no joke or courtly fiction. Roger Ascham used it as a cudgel for the idle wits of the young gentlemen of the day: "It is your shame (I speak to you all, you young gentlemen of England) that one maid should go beyond you all in excel-

lency of learning and knowledge of divers tongues. Point
forth six of the best given gentlemen of this court, and all
they together show not so much good will, spend not so
much time, bestow not so many hours, daily, orderly, and
constantly, for the increase of learning and knowledge as
doth the Queen's majesty herself. Yea, I believe that, beside her perfect readiness in Latin, Italian, French, and
Spanish, she readeth here now at Windsor more Greek
every day than some prebendary of this church doth Latin
in a whole week."

When her brother Edward died, in 1553, Elizabeth had
fifty years more to live. The first five of these, during the
reign of Mary, were spent in the acquirement of tenacity,
tact, and worldly wisdom; and then—for over forty-
four years—she ruled. Hardly was Mary seated on the
throne when Elizabeth was implicated in the Wyatt rebel-
lion, cross-examined and bullied, carried a prisoner to the
Tower of London, and "ignominiously conducted through
the Traitor's Gate." They got nothing out of her, and
finally sent her to prison at Woodstock. Thence they
dragged her back to court—at the suggestion of King
Philip, it is said—and plagued her with demands that she
change her religion. Elizabeth dissimulated, conciliated,
and remained firm. One of the scenes reads like "Hamlet":

"One night, when it was late, the Princess was unex-
pectedly summoned and conducted by torchlight to the
Queen's bedchamber; where she kneeled down before the
Queen, declaring herself to be a most faithful and true
subject. She even went so far as to request the Queen to
send her some Catholic treatises, which might confirm her
faith and inculcate doctrines different from those which
she had been taught in the writings of the Reformers. The
Queen seemed still to suspect her sincerity, but they parted
on good terms. During this critical interview Philip had
concealed himself behind the tapestry, that he might have

seasonably interposed to prevent the violence of the Queen's passionate temper from proceeding to any extremities."

There were gentlemen behind the arras before Polonius. A week later Elizabeth was freed from most of her guards and permitted to retire to Hatfield, where she was astutely living when Queen Mary died. They who would learn to rule must first learn to obey. Imperious as Queen Elizabeth often showed herself to her subjects, the obedience she demanded was but child's play in comparison with that which she had herself rendered, with imperturbable tact and good humor, during the three arbitrary and inconsistent reigns in which she grew up and acquired the lessons of discipline.

She was crowned in London, at the age of twenty-five, on January 14, 1559. Since her predecessor's death a month had been passed at Hatfield and in a leisurely progress to Westminster, and another month in preparation there. On the twelfth of January she crossed the Rubicon, or, in the language of the day, "shot London Bridge"—that is, negotiated the dangerous arches. Holinshed brings this scene also to life:

"On Thursday, the twelfth of January, the Queen's majesty removed from her palace of Westminster by water unto the Tower of London. The Lord Mayor and aldermen in their barge, and all the citizens with their barges decked and trimmed with targets and banners of their mysteries, accordingly attend on her Grace. The bachelors' barge of the Lord Mayor's company—to wit, the mercers—had their barge with a foist [light galley] trimmed with three tops, and artillery aboard, gallantly appointed to wait upon them, shooting off lustily as they went with great and pleasant melody of instruments, which played in most sweet and heavenly manner. Her Grace shot the Bridge about two of the clock in the afternoon, at the still of the ebb, the Lord Mayor and the rest following after her barge, attending the same, till her Majesty took land at the privy stairs at the Tower Wharf."

Magnificent pageantry and every indication of genuine popular enthusiasm accompanied her coronation journey through London. Nor did her subjects omit the opportunity to point out to her allegorically the way in which they wished her to walk. "In a pageant erected near the Little Conduit in the upper end of Cheapside, an old man with a scythe and wings, representing Time, appeared, coming out of a hollow place or cave, leading another person all clad in white silk, gracefully apparelled, who represented Truth (the daughter of Time); which lady had a book in her hand, on which was written *Verbum Veritatis*, i.e., The Word of Truth. It was the Bible in English: which, after a speech made to the queen, Truth reached down towards her, which was taken and brought by a gentleman attending to her hands. As soon as she received it, she kissed it, and with both her hands held it up, and then laid it upon her breast, greatly thanking the City for that present, and said, *She would often read over that Book.*"

At this point she received also a purse containing a thousand marks in gold, in which case the intervention of the attending gentleman appears to have been unnecessary, for, we are told, "The Queen's majesty with both her hands took the purse," and answered the giver "marvelous pithily, and so pithily that the standers by, as they embraced entirely her gracious answer, so they marveled at the couching thereof, which was in words truly reported these:

" 'I thank my Lord Mayor, his brethren, and you all. And whereas your request is that I should continue your good Lady and Queen, be ye ensured that I will be as good unto you as ever Queen was to her people. No will in me can lack, neither do I trust shall there lack any power. And persuade yourselves that for the safety and quietness of you all I will not spare, if need be, to spend my blood. God thank you all!' "

Meantime she gave herself up to showy public entertainments, which after the gloom of Mary's reign pleased the Londoners as much as they satisfied the queen's Renaissance tastes. On the following St. George's Day, April 23, she supped at the residence of the Earl of Pembroke; "and after supper she took a boat and was rowed up and down in the River Thames." For a time the staid metropolis became a second Venice, "hundreds of boats and barges rowing about her, and thousands of people thronging at the waterside to look upon her Majesty: rejoicing to see her, and partaking of the music and sights on the Thames; for the trumpets blew, drums beat, flutes played, guns were discharged, squibs hurled up into the air, as the Queen moved from place to place. And this continued till ten of the clock at night, when the Queen departed home. By these means, showing herself so freely and condescendingly unto her people, she made herself dear and acceptable unto them."

It was a merry England while she reigned. Plays flourished, as we know, and music was more native to the soil than ever since. One of her Puritanical subjects, writing in Latin, ventured to speak of her in 1563 as consuming days and nights in flirtations, hunting, hawking, choral shows, and ludicrous entertainments ("choreis et rebus ludicris"). A Spanish report, nearly forty years later, contains one sardonic sentence which may well have raised a wonder in Castilian minds beyond even what the Armada had instilled: "The head of the Church of England and Ireland was to be seen in her old age dancing three or four galliards."

Deerslaying, with crossbow and arrow, was a major pas-

sion; and those whom she delighted to honor profited by
the fruits of her marksmanship—though often (as was
usual when she condescended) not without embarrass-
ment. Her loyal henchman, Robin of Leicester, was rather
put to it when commanded to deliver to Archbishop
Parker of Canterbury a stag she had killed at Windsor
on a hot September second. The ingenious Dudley
met the situation like a statesman, and thus he writes to
Parker:

"My Lord: The Queen's Majesty being abroad hunting yesterday in the forest, and having had very good hap
besides great sport, she hath thought good to remember
your Grace with part of her prey, and so commanded me
to send you from her Highness a great and fat stag killed
with her own hand; which, because the weather was hot,
and the deer somewhat chafed and dangerous to be carried
so far without some help, I caused him to be *parboiled* in
this sort for the better preservation of him—which I doubt
not but shall cause him to come unto you as I would be
glad he should." If no longer handsome, we may hope that
the queen's gift was still worthy the digestion of an archbishop when he arrived.

Elizabeth's bashfulness was famous and unique. Young
Gilbert Talbot, son of the Earl of Shrewsbury, wrote to
his father of an episode that occurred on the May Day
when the queen was forty-four and Gilbert twenty-four:
"In the morning, about eight of the clock, I happened to
walk in the tilt-yard, under the gallery where her Majesty
useth to stand to see the running at tilt; where by chance
she was, and looking out of the window; my eye was
full towards her, and she showed to be greatly ashamed
thereof, for that she was unready and in her night-stuff.
So when she saw me at after dinner, as she went to walk,
she gave me a great fillip on the forehead and told my
Lord Chamberlain, who was the next to her, how I had

seen her that morning, and how much ashamed thereof she was."

There can be no question that Gilbert loved the old lady ever after, nor doubted that she was every inch a queen. The mottoes that Spenser places around the walls of Busirane's castle were what Elizabeth taught all Englishmen to see about her presence: "Be bold!" "Be bold!" "*Be not too bold!*" The one certain thing is that her subjects loved her, and that, indeed, to love her was a liberal education.

Temptingly formidable at home, Elizabeth was doubly so when she traveled—and she traveled, of course, incessantly, though she was never off English soil. Her "progresses" were not the least ingenious development of her statesmanship. They amounted to a supertax, by which the wealthy contributed to the expenses of the court; for regular taxes under Elizabeth were moderate and by no means rigorously collected. What more was needed for governmental purposes was largely defrayed by the remarkable succession of public-spirited men to whom she entrusted the direction of the various departments. The excess cost of maintaining the royal court itself came from the well-filled purses of the nobles and gentry among whom she "progressed" some six months in the year. It was hard work for the queen, this gypsy life, though she did it *con amore;* but it taught her to know England from Dover to Berwick, and it inevitably brought culture and a sense of public affairs into the citadels of Bourbon insularity.

Of course the country magnates, whose hospitality the queen and her multitudinous court elected to enjoy, were beset by many emotions. There was pride over the distinction conferred, anxiety over the success of the visit, inward ruefulness at thought of what the entertainment would cost, and loud exclamations over the difficulties of assembling enough food for the throng. When Lord Buckhurst, author of *Gorboduc*, a considerable favorite of Elizabeth and one of the wealthiest men in England, apprehended a visit in 1577, he was moved to write in terms like these to the Lord Chamberlain, who arranged the details of the progresses: "That he beseeched his Lordship to pardon him that he became troublesome unto him, to know some certainty of the Progress, if it might possibly be; the time of provision was so short and the desire he had to do all things in such sort as appertained so great, as he could not but thus importune his Lordship to procure her Highness to grow to some resolution, both of the time when her Majesty would be at Lewes, and how long her Highness would stay there. For that, he having already sent into Kent, Surrey, and Sussex for provision, he assured his Lordship he found all places possessed by my Lord of Arundel, my Lord Montagu, and others [that is, other expectant and foresighted hosts]; so as of force he was to send into Flanders, which he would speedily do, if the time of her Majesty's coming and tarriance with him were certain."

Nichols, the guileless Georgian laureate of Elizabeth's progresses, introduces this with the statement: "The Lord Buckhurst in particular was very desirous to entertain her at his house in Sussex." Was he? Henry Goring, Esq., of Burton in Sussex, writes in unconcealed apprehension to his old friend, Sir William More of Loseley, that, "hearing the Queen has lain two nights at Loseley, and intended to lie two nights at his house in Sussex," he wishes to know how he is to entertain her; "whether she brings her own stuff, beer, and other provisions, or whether Sir William provided every part." The answer doubtless was that ordinarily the queen provided very little, though she did show, on the whole, a judicious discrimination in her demands and knew how to temper the wind of her favor to the shorn host.

It is said that when Queen Victoria visited her subjects—far more rarely, and less numerously attended—a chief object of anxiety was the quality of the royal rice pudding. With Elizabeth it was the beer that made most trouble. When she visited Cambridge in 1564, she was so much pleased by the academic entertainment that she stayed a day longer than had been intended; "and a saying was, if provision of beer and ale could have been made, her Grace would have remained till Friday." On another occasion the beer was found unsatisfactory, and the resulting displeasure excited her *fidus Achates*, Leicester, out of all care for his h's. "Hit," as he reported to Burghley, "did put her very far out of temper, and almost all the company beside." However, a better brew had been discovered, and "God be thanked, she is now perfectly well and merry."

The *Sayings of Queen Elizabeth*, lately collected by Mr. Chamberlin, are in part as apocryphal, doubtless, as the once famous *Sayings of King Alfred*; but there are some which are authentically documented and have the authentic ring. Thus she admonished her judges: "Have a care over my people. You have my people: do you that which I ought to do. They are my people. Every man oppresseth and spoileth them without mercy: they cannot revenge their quarrel nor help themselves. See unto them; see unto them, for they are my charge. I charge you, even as God hath charged me. I care not for myself: my life is not dear to me; my care is for my people. I pray God, whosoever succeedeth me be as careful of them as I am."

To Philip the Second she is reported to have written concerning his rebellious Dutch subjects: "What does it matter to your Majesty, if they go to the devil in their own way?" Her vanity, intellectuality, and heroism are all illustrated by the words she is said to have spoken to the Archbishop of St. Andrew's, when the Scots were threatening her: "I am more afraid of making a fault in my Latin than of the Kings of Spain, France, Scotland, the whole House of Guise, and all of their confederates."

And so she passes down the ages, not perhaps the imperial votaress that Shakespeare saw "in maiden meditation fancy-free," but surely as fascinating and inscrutable as Mona Lisa. She has been charged with all the moral and political vices—with nearly all the frailties of her sex and species. All her good qualities, except her courage and her love of the English people, can be plausibly impugned; but nothing can yet be proved against her.

A woman who for seventy years stood on as slippery footing as mortals have often trod, at the most perilous post in one of the most perilous ages of the world, exposed to the scandal, intrigues, and prying, not of a nation, but of a continent—the ambiguous queen continues to smile down the truth of Antony's saying,

> The evil that men do lives after them,
> The good is oft interred with their bones.

The good that Elizabeth did has not yet been interred with her bones: the unexampled achievements of her reign are still the heritage of her nation and one of the truisms of history. Ten years after she was dead and buried, when an alien dynasty was settled on her throne, John Fletcher (in the play called Shakespeare's *Henry VIII*) dramatized the scene of her baptism with which I began this essay, and he put into the mouth of the officiating Archbishop a prophetic recapitulation of the queen's achievements:

> . . . Let me speak, sir,
> For Heaven now bids me; and the words I utter
> Let none think flattery, for they'll find 'em truth.
> This royal infant—Heaven still move about her!—
> Though in her cradle, yet now promises
> Upon this land a thousand thousand blessings,

Which time shall bring to ripeness. . . .
She shall be lov'd and fear'd: her own shall bless her;
Her foes shake like a field of beaten corn,
And hang their heads with sorrow. Good grows with her.
In her days every man shall eat in safety,
Under his own vine, what he plants, and sing
The merry songs of peace to all his neighbours.

If Elizabeth did evil, it is so far from living after her that
to this day the suspicion of it has not crept beyond the
twilit limbo of discredited gossip. Froude employed volumes in an effort to disprove her greatness as a sovereign,
to present her as a meddling and inconstant marplot, hin-
dering the schemes of her great agents, Burghley, Walsingham, and Drake. And for this, most of all his sins, the
brilliant and captivating Froude is today rejected of historians. If Elizabeth lacked political wisdom, one may
well ask by what unparalleled luck did she keep herself
surrounded by such a succession of able ministers, so ardu-
ously and self-sacrificingly zealous in working out her
policies? To explain why none who knew her doubted
her fitness for her throne, one need but quote a couple
more of her sayings. When Parliament was eager to force
its policies upon her, she answered: "I am your anointed
Queen. I will never be by violence constrained to do *anything*. I thank God, I am endued with such qualities that
if I were turned out of the Realm in my petticoat, I were
able to live in any place in Christendom." And to one of
the sanest and truest of her servants, the Lord Keeper
Bacon, she remarked in the difficult middle years of her
reign: "I have followed your advice, these two years past,
in all the affairs of my kingdom, and I have seen nothing
but trouble, expense, and danger. From this hour, for the
same length of time, I am going to follow my own opinion,
and see if I find I do any better." It hardly matters whether
or not we can today prove that these were indeed the

great queen's *ipsissima verba:* it is enough that they were the words which the age that knew her best thought it characteristic of her to utter.

Elizabeth's love affairs and flirtations were always notorious, and were meant to be so. They were part of her nature and part of her diplomacy. There was the strange girlhood affair with Admiral Seymour, and the succeeding affairs with Leicester, Alençon, Ralegh, Essex, and Hatton. One would like to believe her unchaste in order to believe her human, in order to lessen the oppressiveness of her mystery. In logic, she must have been. How singular that all the public inquiry she was perpetually challenging, all the private papers of foreign ambassadors and spies, and all the research of historians have left the hypothesis of her virginity still unrefuted! Mr. Frederick Chamberlin, whose examination into the *Private Character of Queen Elizabeth* has recently aroused some interests, admits that he began his studies with extraordinarily liberal assumptions of guilt. "I had never doubted," he says, "that Elizabeth was the mistress of Leicester, of Essex, of Ralegh, of Hatton, &c." His investigations, however, forced him to a surprising change of front, resulting in the conclusion that Elizabeth had been virtuous because of lifelong debility. Debility, indeed! Another biologic endorsement of the queen's purity, more credible in character, figures in the gossip with which Ben Jonson entertained Drummond of Hawthornden in 1618; but the merest gossip it remains, unfounded and unlikely, though natural enough to be invented out of the circumstance of her celibacy. The opinion of good historians, which was voiced over twenty years ago at the conclusion of Mr. Martin Hume's book on the *Courtships of Queen Elizabeth*, still stands: "All the love affairs that we have glanced at in their non-political aspect were but the solace of a great governing genius, who was supremely vain. Though they were accompanied by circumstances which were reprehensible, undignified and indelicate for any virtuous woman, much less a Queen, the arguments and evidence that I have been able to adduce should lead, in my opinion, to the delivery of a verdict of non-proven on the generally believed main charge against the Queen of actual immorality."

And so again she eludes us. The Virgin Queen! The despair of skeptics, the shame of the historical mudslinger. After three centuries, and despite some of the worst atrocities of modern historiography, her queenliness remains, and her virginity is still—where it was. With whom are we to match her? With whom but with the man of Stratford, the greatest of all her subjects, her mightiest colleague in building the age we know alternatively by both their names? Shakespeare, too, stands garbed in dubiety, fretted and pursued by modern Guildensterns, who would fain uncrown him, "would seem to know" his "stops," "would pluck out the heart of" his "mystery." At the end there are no better words to apply to Elizabeth than those Arnold addressed to her poet:

> Others abide our question. Thou art free.
> We ask and ask: Thou smilest and art still,
> Out-topping knowledge.

SHAKESPEARE APART

THE greatest of the Elizabethan romanticists is neither so conspicuously Elizabethan nor so transparently romantic as most of his contemporaries. Shakespeare's difference from his fellows is apparent, indeed, in the difficulty we encounter when we seek adjectives to qualify his work. For Spenser and Marlowe, Sidney and Ralegh, it is not so hard to find expressive and satisfying characterizations; the critic of Shakespeare is thrown back upon paradox. The greatest English writer is in many ways one of the least literary; the most brilliant constructor of plot, one of the least inventive; the most successful searcher of the human heart, one of the least subtle. Shakespeare was neither an artist in the sense in which Spenser was, nor a romanticist as Ralegh was, nor an intellectualist as Marlowe was. Wisdom is perhaps the only attribute which we can apply to him without need of qualification.

And Shakespeare's wisdom was not of the kind which colleges supply. We need no biographical evidence to assure us that the author of the plays was not indebted to the universities; and the academic attitude on the part of his critics has often proved the least profitable of all. Ben Jonson and Samuel Johnson and Dryden, for example, have said splendidly true things of Shakespeare when they spoke, unofficially as it were, from the depth of their robust humanity; and each has been signally unfortunate when essaying to write of him from the chair of a literary dictator. The clearest light on this poet has often emanated not from academic halls but from the experience of those who have rather taken degrees in what old Gower calls the University of all the world—in Shakespeare's university. The Welsh private gentleman Maurice Morgann (author of the vindication of Falstaff), Lamb, Hazlitt, Dr. Furnivall, and Dr. Furness—all very unacademic men—have been among the quickest to discern the essential greatnesses of Shakespeare.

A chief reason why formal criticism has proved so barren is simply that Shakespeare—more even than most other romantic writers—attained his art by indirection. A straight line, indeed, is seldom the shortest line between a romantic poet's inspiration and his accomplishment; but in Shakespeare the usual Elizabethan carelessness about rules of poetry may often seem magnified into carelessness about poetry itself. "The works of Shakespeare," says Coleridge, "are romantic poetry revealing itself in the drama." But his romanticism requires to be distinguished from that of his great contemporaries. In the sense that the romanticist is one who ignores academic rules for writing, Shakespeare is a very type and pattern of the romantic dramatist; but he has nothing of that other, more advanced, romanticism which marks Spenser and Marlowe as conscious innovators and revolutionists, battling for ideas which they know to be strange and love therefor. He has nothing of the romanticism which produced *Hernani*. Shakespeare's romanticism did not lead him to affect originality or to despise precedent; nor did it impel him to establish new rules for dramatic writing. Mr. Munro hardly exaggerates when he says in the preface to the *Shakespeare Allusion Book*: "Shakespeare, like all the great poets of the world, left no school behind him. He was not an initiator; he invented no new style; he introduced no new vogue."

Shakespeare was constitutionally incapable of doing what Lyly, Marlowe, and Ben Jonson successively did—of inventing a perfectly characteristic new type of drama and then consistently illustrating it in his practice. Probably he would have been incapable of offering concerning the dramatist's art any views as definite as Hamlet expresses about the actor's. What he created in the way of dramatic style and structure—and it was, of course, a great deal—seems to have come to him as the result of practice rather than speculation. What he borrowed—and it was even more—found its way into his plays by chance more often than by critical choice. In the controversy between classic and romantic theories of drama—between Jonson's method and Marlowe's—Shakespeare seems to take no stand and feel no interest. It happens that two particularly romantic plays, *The Tempest* and *Othello*, are in their structure nearly as classic (regular) as two of Jonson's, while two plays of classic atmosphere and story, *Julius Caesar* and *Antony and Cleopatra*, carry to the farthest extreme the romantic irregularities. For these things—for the whole formal side of poetry—Shakespeare doubtless cared as little as Homer. Like Homer, he can hardly be designated as either romantic or classic; and more than any other modern he has succeeded in making his art seem coextensive with life, in arrogating to himself Pope's fine claim for Homer:

To follow nature is to follow him.

It is the indirectness of Shakespeare's art that here accounts for its wonderful success. The perfectly clear light in which his men and women are seen implies a perfect lack of self-consciousness in their portrayer, and this we can very safely credit him with. Shakespeare was in no way a critic. His taste in books does not seem to have been good, if we may judge by some of the poor works he chooses to dramatize and by the many great ones he ignores. Compared with his most worthy contemporaries, Shakespeare rather lacked the literary conscience. Compared, that is, with Lyly, Marlowe, or Jonson, he was not more, but less careful in choosing and developing his plot, in shaping his sentences, and in winding up his conclusions.

Had Shakespeare been the sort of man that he is thought to have been by those who identify him with Francis or with Anthony Bacon, or with Ralegh, or with Marlowe, or with Rutland or Southampton, or with Edward de Vere, Earl of Oxford, or with William Stanley, Earl of Derby—that is, had he been well bred and college trained, all this we may feel sure, would have been different. He would have been more precocious and more clever. In all human probability he would have been much less wise. He would have been more fastidious about accuracy of detail in sentence structure, in plot construction, and in plausibility of incident and local color. He would have sought the appearance of originality more and attained the substance less.

One great strength of Shakespeare's dramatic art lies in the fact that circumstances made him a great connoisseur of life and a very careless student of literature. He was first an actor, second a practical adapter of old plays, third a company manager. Only fourth and last was he a dramatist proper. No other Elizabethan writer had so many and such intimate points of contact with the whole business of the theater. A very important reason for Shakespeare's superiority to his contemporaries is that he was not primarily a gentleman author like Lyly, Greene, Peele, Marlowe, but actually, as Greene called him, "an absolute Johannes factotum" of the theater, a man too absorbed in opening the world's oyster—in holding the mirror up to life—to feel much the littlenesses and compunctions of the artist.

From these general, and rather trite, remarks two truths can be deduced. One is that Shakespeare is not, as he seems often to be thought, the summation of Elizabethan literary art. The student of Shakespeare will know much of human nature but not a vast deal about the sixteenth-century mind. Shakespeare was indeed *not* of one age, and did not supersede Lyly and Spenser and Marlowe and Jonson as exponents of his era.

The other truth is that the problems of Shakespeare's great plays are not to be settled triumphantly by frontal literary attack, by disquisitions upon his mind and art alone. The personality of Shakespeare has been so dismally disputed that students have sometimes been driven to wish the whole matter buried in Cimmerian gloom. Thus Dr. Furness attempts to lighten ship by merrily bidding the man Shakespeare begone with all his mystery:

"It is merely our ignorance which creates the mystery. To Shakespeare's friends and daily companions there was nothing mysterious in his life; on the contrary, it possibly appeared to them as unusually dull and commonplace. It certainly had no incidents so far out of the common that they thought it worth while to record them. Shakespeare never killed a man as Jonson did; his voice was never heard, like Marlowe's, in tavern brawls; nor was he ever, like Marston and Chapman, threatened with the penalty of having his ears lopped and his nose slit; but his life was so gentle and so clear in the sight of man and of Heaven that no record of it has come down to us; for which failure I am fervently grateful, and as fervently hope that no future year will ever reveal even the faintest peep through the divinity which doth hedge this king."

Unfortunately, it is precisely the man Shakespeare—in some circles derisively called the Stratfordian—who carries with him into obscurity the dramatic artist. Without him—ill bred, ill lettered, and in some ways, perhaps, ill balanced as he was—the plays lose their coherent meaning and disintegrate into picture puzzles, in which mad ladies and gentlemen piece out the names and features of whom they will.

There was once a time when it seemed a mark of daring and original thought to assert the identity of Francis Bacon with the author of the Shakespearean dramas. That time is now past and the mere Baconian is in sorry plight. His doctrine is as hackneyed as that of the Shakespearean and it lacks the compensating satisfaction of reason. There are few joys in being illogical when one must also be flat. Desperate cases produce desperate remedies, and super-Baconians have lately arisen, ready to supplant the pale ineffectual fires of their predecessors by yet brighter blazes of assumption.

Of late years, however, the preachers of Shakespearean dissent have manifested a tendency to abandon Bacon in order to exploit newer aspirants to the laurel. The revelation of Mr. J. C. Nicol, in *The Real Shakespeare*, is couched in mystical language: "I, Fortinbras, otherwise Posthumus, quarried and on 7th December, 1905, plainly discovered Henry Wriotheslie, third Earl of Southampton, undoubtedly to be the sole Author and begetter of the so-called poems and plays known as Shakespeare's Works . . . producing innumerable offspring in Art, with other various names, notably (as Marlowe) from the age of 13." A contemporary work by Peter Alvor, *Das neue Shakespeare-Evangelium*, ascribes Shakespeare to a judicious partnership between the Earls of Southampton and Rutland. In 1912 M. Célestin Demblon, Socialist Deputy from Liége, maintained through 559 pages the thesis: "Lord Rutland est Shakespeare." In 1914 the late Henry Pemberton, Jr., did as much for Ralegh in *Shakspere and Sir Walter Ralegh*. In 1919 appeared the two impressive volumes of Professor Abel Lefranc, in nomination of another candidate: *Sous le Masque de "William Shakespeare": William Stanley VIe Comte de Derby;* and in 1920 the most portentous perhaps of all these colossal works, Mr. J. Thomas Looney's *"Shakespeare"*

Identified in Edward de Vere, the Seventeenth Earl of Oxford.

The desire to see the face behind the mask is not only legitimate but necessary, and happily it has not recently been exclusively confined to the Bacon-Ralegh-Oxford-Derby-Rutland-Southampton exponents of critical solitaire. The most priceless hour of the irrecoverable past, says Mr. William Archer, would be that in which one might meet the real Shakespeare face to face; and Professor Bradley says: "For my own part I confess that, though I should care nothing about the man if he had not written the works, yet, since we possess them, I would rather see and hear him for five minutes in his proper person than discover a new one." If the efforts of Mr. Frank Harris savor more sometimes of the police court than the study, the last dozen years have produced several studies which are full of help—notably Professor Bradley's lecture on "Shakespeare the Man" and Professor Manly's on "Shakespeare Himself." Is it possible to glean a little after such reapers?

The author of the Shakespearean plays, we can say with perfect confidence, was not the advanced political thinker that Bacon was, or Ralegh, or Spenser, or even Marlowe. He was distinctly a traditionalist in politics and social theory. His attitude toward the state and sovereign was not Tudor but Plantagenet; not Renaissance but feudal. It represents the feeling of Stratford much better than that of London.

The King in Shakespeare is nearly always the man on horseback. He who rides roan Barbary gets the plaudits of the multitude; and Shakespeare's voice can generally be heard among the rest, crying with quite old-fashioned vehemence: "Le Roi est mort; Vive le Roi!" Shakespeare's kings, it has been said, are always kingly—and so they are in the old Plantagenet sense. They go to bed with their crowns on and sleep with the scepter under their pillow. They brandish swords and throw down warders, and make polished speeches which, in a surprising number of the examples, lack moral or psychological sincerity.

Shakespeare's loyalty was always that of the Tory country dweller. No length of years in London, no number of performances at court, sufficed to obliterate the country boy's impression of the vague, exotic splendor of the crown. His is not the personal devotion of the cavalier to Charles, nor the imperial ardor of such typical Elizabethans as Spenser and Ralegh. It is rather the old feudal attitude of the Wars of the Roses, the attitude of the Yorkist who would have fought for the crown of England though he found it on a thistle bush. There is every reason for believing that Shakespeare was quite satisfied with the *de facto* principle of sovereignty which Prince Hal expounds to his father:

> . . . My gracious liege,
> You won it, wore it, kept it, gave it me.
> Then plain and right must my possession be.

Perhaps it is not altogether an accident that in Shakespeare's biography the careless continuators of the old feudal England—Southampton and Essex and Pembroke—mean a great deal, and the purveyors of the new political faith—Burghley, Ralegh, and Walsingham—mean nothing.

Shakespeare's patriotism also, glowing though it is, is traditional and essentially pre-Elizabethan. He has nothing of the new imperialism so dominant in Ralegh and Spenser, and very little indeed of the sense of the gorgeous Indies and the new world beyond the seas that Marlowe shows everywhere. He was distinctly a "little Englander." He glories in the thought of the aloofness and self-sufficiency of his island,

> . . . this sceptred isle,
> This earth of majesty, this seat of Mars,
> This other Eden, demi-Paradise,
> This fortress built by Nature for herself.

His vision stops at the ideal of a hermit kingdom, free from foreign entanglements, safe in the unity of its citizens and in a proudly defensive attitude toward the world:

> This England never did, nor never shall,
> Lie at the proud foot of a conqueror,
> But when it first did help to wound itself.
> Now these her princes are come home again,
> Come the three corners of the world in arms,
> And we shall shock them.

Wars abroad are for him but sallies from the fortress, heroic yet of dubious advisability. Henry the Fifth has legalistic but no imperial aims, and Agincourt is particularly glorified as a defensive action. Says Henry to Montjoy:

> . . . Turn thee back,
> And tell thy king I do not seek him now,
> But could be willing to march on to Calais
> Without impeachment.

The jingoes, pray observe, are all in the French camp— all but Captain MacMorris the Irishman, who by Gower's account (and his own) is "a very valiant gentleman" and a fire-eater, and for whom we have Fluellen's unimpeachable authority that "he is an ass, as in the world: I will verify as much in his peard: he has no more directions in the two disciplines of the wars, look you, . . . than is a puppy-dog."

There is more of zeal for national expansion and aggressive foreign policy in the one play of *Edward III* (I think, by Peele) than in all that Shakespeare wrote.

The very sea, which to Ralegh and Spenser ever was beckoning Englishmen abroad, which was Cynthia's peculiar domain and highway, is to Shakespeare a defensive wall, a moat, whose purpose was to shut off the alien lands from

> . . . this little world,
> This precious stone set in the silver sea,
> Which serves it in the office of a wall,
> Or as a moat defensive to a house.

The England he apostrophizes is not the mistress of the ocean but

> England bound in with the triumphant sea,
> Whose rocky shore beats back the envious siege
> Of watery Neptune.

There is nothing that would justify us in assuming that Shakespeare's heart e'er within him burned with desire to board a seagoing vessel, or that he ever cared to join the Elizabethan crowds which flocked to visit Drake's *Golden Hind* at Deptford.

The prejudices of the country-bred youth persist also in Shakespeare's treatment of the various classes of English society. He has the old-fashioned rustic's fondness for lords and ladies and for country squires, and for all the functionaries that go in their train: footmen and porters, hostlers, tapsters, gardeners, and pedlars. (Note the groom in *Richard II*.) The plain tiller of the soil gets loving treatment, from Costard in *Love's Labour's Lost* to the charming Egyptian clown in *Antony and Cleopatra*; and he offers conspicuous homage to the Cotswold shepherds in *As You Like It* and in *The Winter's Tale*.

The denizens of the city, on the other hand—with honorable exception of the tavern drawers—seldom evoke Shakespeare's interest. The Lord Mayor and aldermen, the livery companies, law clerks, and apprentices, the

Puritan sectaries, and cutpurses, and street singers—all the picturesque and bizarrely differentiated types that made up the pride, pomp, and circumstance, as well as the bustle and romantic uncertainties, of Elizabethan London— whom Dekker painted so lovingly and Jonson with such microscopic fidelity—are by Shakespeare referred to little and dispraisingly. The "velvet guards and Sunday citizens" and the whole shopkeeping class, from the apothecary in *Romeo and Juliet* down, arouse at best his pity and almost invariably his scorn. They are used most to barb the point of his contemptuous metaphors. The rude mechanicals or city artisans are dull and pompous, and the great body of citizens is the *mobile vulgus* and nothing more, an object equally of derision and distrust.

A single striking example may illustrate the point. There was one rough, roystering, and unique set of Londoners who must have come under constant observation of a man doing business on the Bankside. It was the tribe of watermen or scullers, a body numbering its hundreds, if not thousands, and possessed even of its laureate in Taylor the Water-Poet. Indisputably Shakespeare must have sat tête-à-tête with dozens of them on the way to Southwark, and his fortune can hardly have been so bad that he met only the dull dogs in so hilarious a fraternity. Yet he never came nearer to a tribute than when in *Othello* he let drop his casual slur on

A knave of common hire, a gondolier.

Are we not almost justified in thinking that the well-styled Bard of *Avon* (not Thames) was the converse of Peter Bell? A primrose by the water's brim was to Shakespeare all that it was to Wordsworth, but the delectable Taylor was to him, I sadly fear, simply "a knave of common hire," and he was nothing more. We may find in this a reason why Shakespeare never chose to write a city comedy. Here again, then, there is in Shakespeare more of Stratford than of London, more of Plantagenet than of Tudor England.

In religion also Shakespeare evidently did not feel the attraction of the new ideas which so appealed to Spenser, Marlowe, and Ralegh. There is no good reason for believing that he was an actual recusant, a convinced disciple of the Roman faith; but the religious penumbra of his mind was certainly archaic. For poetic purposes at least religion still connoted for him friars, masses, vigils, extreme unction, and purgatory. It came natural to him to invoke angels and ministers of grace, to swear by Our Lady and Saint Patrick.

The reader, therefore, who knows only Shakespeare among the Elizabethans will get relatively very little of the intellectual atmosphere in which Milton and other Londoners of the next generation grew up. He will get less of this from Shakespeare than from any other eminent writer of the period.

The greatest of modern poets passed a quarter century amid the tremendous intellectual currents—social, religious, and imperial—of Elizabethan London, and his soul through all this time remained a stranger to them. "Multum incola fuit anima sua." His most apparent efforts to reflect the spirit around him are the relative failures of *Love's Labour's Lost* and *The Merry Wives of Windsor*. He gave his audiences, to be sure, what they liked immensely, but he gave it with a strange and stubborn indirectness. The Armada comes and goes; Drake and Ralegh light the beacons of a new and potent patriotism; and Shakespeare tunes his native woodland harp to sing, in *Henry V*, the praises of an obsolete Lancastrian policy. Great Britain has its birth in the union of Scotland and England, and Shakespeare weaves into *Macbeth* a musty dynastic compliment to the new monarch.

The London bookstalls groan with pamphlets about the discovery of Bermuda and the colonization of Virginia, about cannibals and noble savages, and the Isle of Devils and the Fountain of Perpetual Youth. Drayton writes his ecstatic stanzas "To the Virginian Voyage." In the play of *Eastward Hoe* even the gravity of Chapman, the local realism of Jonson and Marston, succumb to the infection; and in the speeches of Captain Seagull this comedy of London manners grows iridescent with fanciful hyperboles of Virginian opportunity. Spenser's vision leaps from East to Western Ind, dilating on "Th' Indian Peru," "The Amazon's huge river," or "fruitfullest Virginia"; invoking ceaselessly

> . . . the beaten marinere,
> That long hath wandred in the Ocean wide,
> Oft soust in swelling Tethys saltish teare,
> And long time having tand his tawny hide
> With blustring breath of heaven that none can bide.

In Marlowe, Tamburlaine dreams of

> East India and the late discover'd Isles,

Barabas of

> . . . the merchants of the Indian Mines,
> That trade in metal of the purest mould,

and Faustus of the "huge argosies" that drag

> . . . from America the golden fleece,
> That yearly stuffs old Philip's treasury.

Shakespeare never mentions Virginia and names America only once, in the early *Comedy of Errors*. Once, in a bit of comic prose, he lets Maria allude with betraying carelessness to "the new map with the augmentation of the Indies." Contrast the inspirational potency of maps and globes for Marlowe, Hakluyt, and Spenser! Finally Shakespeare offers belated and grudging acquiescence to the spirit of discovery by telling (in his last play) how a Duke of Milan and his daughter once went sailing on the Mediterranean in

> A rotten carcass of a boat; not rigg'd,
> Nor tackle, sail, nor mast,

(a boat for Shakespeare is most often simply something to get wrecked in; he does not use horses so!)—and how they found there an enchanted isle—forsooth, not far from Tunis and Algiers!

Shakespeare did not bring with him from Stratford a very plastic, or, as we should say, a trained, mind. He brought limitations and prejudices which he never outgrew. He also brought three things that matter more: an unaccountable genius; a tremendous capacity for hard work; and an extraordinary interest in men and women, based on a various, and not impeccable experience of them.

He did not bring with him, as Horatio did (or said he did), a truant disposition, but one already fixed in the course it must pursue. Undoubtedly the emotionalist and the thinker had at one time struggled within him: Richard the Second with Bolingbroke, Romeo with Mercutio, Hotspur with Falstaff. Undoubtedly the time had been when emotion had held sway, and Shakespeare was both a sadder and a wiser man thereby. But that time, we may be sure, was over before ever Shakespeare saw London and commenced dramatist. In all that he wrote for the stage, in the sonnets too, and even in the poems, which Hazlitt likens to "a couple of ice-houses . . . as hard, as glittering, and as cold," thought and reflection transcend emotion. From Biron in *Love's Labour's Lost* to Prospero in *The Tempest*, Shakespeare elaborates the principle that thought is the very core of life and feeling but its outer husk. "There's nothing either good or bad but thinking makes it so." His two greatest figures, the two who are most truly representative of him, Hamlet and Falstaff, are men of thought, not men of feeling, and not men of action. So in their different ways are Ulysses and Brutus, Henry the Fifth and Iago. In Cleopatra he paints not the witchery that inflames the passions but that which unhinges the intellect. It is the Serpent, not the Siren, that he sees, and Antony sums her up in the words:

> She is *cunning* past man's *thought*.

Where Marlowe pictures human aspiration as resulting from the clash of unresting and irreconcilable emotions, and declares:

> Nature that framed us of four elements,
> Still warring in our breasts for regiment . . .
> Wills us to wear ourselves and never rest,

Shakespeare views human character as the quiet consequence of the "godlike reason" of the thinking animal:

> Sure, he that made us with such large discourse,
> Looking before and after, gave us not
> That capability and godlike reason
> To fust in us unused.

It is again the thinking side of man that Hamlet stresses in the words which better than any others explain what attracted Shakespeare to the study of human psychology: "What a piece of work is a man! How noble in reason! how infinite in faculty! . . . in apprehension how like a god!" Shakespeare was as comparatively little interested in concrete incident as he was in abstract emotion. The overt act generally has no special significance for him. He was no pragmatist, as Bacon was, and would never have agreed with Bacon that "good thoughts (though God accept them) yet towards men are little better than good dreams, except they be put in act."

The spectrum of life, running from dreams through thoughts into acts, was for the true Elizabethans brightest at the two ends. It was the glory and the weakness alike of Sidney, Spenser, and Ralegh, of Tamburlaine and Faustus, that they saw gorgeous emotional dreams passing directly into brilliant acts. The Scythian Shepherd speaks for them all when he says:

> . . . I am strongly mov'd
> That if I should desire the Persian crown,
> I could attain it with a wondrous ease.

Their imaginations, in truth, were all clad in seven-league boots and made but one careless step of the whole way from the violet of the earliest vision to the blood red of final accomplishment. It especially distinguishes Shakespeare that he kept his eye upon the middle of the spectrum, on that vital and revealing "interim" (between the red and the violet) of which Brutus speaks,

> Between the acting of a dreadful thing
> And the first motion.

The deeds themselves mattered much less to Shakespeare. It is doubtful whether he would have cared to consider whether Hamlet actually did too little or Othello too much. Play after play shows in the carelessness of its closing scenes how rapidly his interest cooled when all the good thinking was over and it remained to reveal the tangible consequences of thought.

So in Shakespeare's actual life he ignored the dreams of El Dorado and imperial England, and he ignored the facts of tobacco and the colonization of Virginia and the Fight of the Revenge, while scrutinizing day by day the thinking minds of the men and women about him. And thereby he gained a wisdom so deep that it concealed his plentiful lack of knowledge—a humanity so immense that few could note how completely he had failed to be Elizabethan.

SHAKESPEARE REMEMBERS HIS YOUTH IN STRATFORD

THE Elizabethans, and Shakespeare among them, habitually saw Italy as a land of high social civilization, where the wealthy classes—however their morals might fester—could at least be sure of suavely perfect service in their homes. The antithesis of all this which one observes in the household of the Capulets at Verona is striking enough to suggest several questions about the play of *Romeo and Juliet*.

We are first struck by the deplorable domestic situation at the Capulets' when (in the second scene) we observe the master of the house entrusting a list of invitations to Sunday supper to a servant so ignorant that he can't read the addresses and so green that he doesn't know how to excuse himself—so naïve also that he doesn't hesitate to add a couple of guests on his own authority. In the next scene the approach of supper brings the whole staff, and indeed the family also, to the verge of hysteria. Says the butler to Lady Capulet:

Madam, the guests are come, supper served up, you called, my young lady asked for, the nurse cursed in the pantry, and everything in extremity. I must hence to wait; I beseech you, follow straight!
Lady Cap. We follow thee! Juliet, the county stays! [Exit running.]

A glimpse into the butler's pantry in scene five shows the servants facing the tasks of removing joint stools, shifting trenchers, and looking to the silver in an agony of noisy desperation. One of the footman's guests, Romeo, inquires Juliet's name of a servant who seems to be so fresh from the employment agency that he hasn't yet identified the family he is working for. On the Tuesday following, the master of the household, planning a modest wedding breakfast for his daughter, despatches one messenger with invitations and another to the "Help for Hire" office: "Sirrah, go hire me twenty cunning cooks." A moment later it develops that there are no servants left in the Capulet mansion, and the master has to carry his own message to the County Paris. At three o'clock the next morning Capulet is frightfully busy in the pantry, bidding Angelica "look to the baked meats" and "spare not for cost," exchanging badinage with the log carrier, and resisting the Nurse's efforts to send him to bed.

Now it is evident that no consideration of tragic art is served by misrepresenting the Capulet family as a group of amiable bounders; and I can think of no honest reply that Shakespeare could have made, if Lord Southampton had asked him why in the world he thought the Capulets lived thus, except "Ignorance, my Lord, pure ignorance."

Steevens suggested something like this long ago in one of his notes, and you will find in the Furness *Variorum* a long record of the snubbing Steevens received—invariably, so far as I have observed:

Steevens turns up his nose aristocratically at Shakespeare for imputing "to an Italian nobleman and his lady all the petty solicitudes of a private house concerning a provincial entertainment"; and he adds very grandly: "To such a bustle our author might have been witness at home; but the like anxieties could not well have occurred in the family of Capulet." Steevens had not well read the history of society (Verplanck, etc.).

It is seldom safe to snub Steevens so lightheartedly; and, at the risk of being snubbed myself, I venture to suggest that the only visible reason for the picture of frontier manners which the domestic scenes of *Romeo and Juliet* portray is that when Shakespeare sketched the background of the tragedy he was by no means so familiar with urbane social life as he was when in 1594 he wrote his friendly dedication of *Lucrece* to Southampton—or even as he was when in 1593 he offered his first timid addresses to that nobleman; in fact, when Shakespeare conceived the play, his most vivid idea of large hospitality *was* what Steevens called "a provincial entertainment"; that is, doubtless, a high bailiff's feast at Stratford.

It is natural to ask how far Capulet, who vitalizes and unifies these scenes of rustic merriment, may be John Shakespeare himself. I do not know, but Capulet emerges as a very living and likeable person, rather surprisingly like the John Shakespeare that we come to know in Mr. Fripp's *Minutes and Accounts of the Corporation of Stratford:* incorrigibly obstinate, and on matters of principle or prejudice impolitic, but generous, solidly beloved by his neighbors, and, for all the risks he took, not unprosperous. At least, he is much closer to this than to the old picture of John phrased by Sir Walter Raleigh: "an energetic, pragmatic, sanguine, frothy man, who was always restlessly scheming and could not make good his gains."

The pseudo-aristocratic background of *Romeo and Juliet* is chiefly supplied by the picture of the Capulet household which I have discussed and by the figure of Mercutio. This last is, of course, one of Shakespeare's great successes, but certain interesting things appear when one examines the materials he has drawn together to create the impression of a gallant and witty nobleman. Mercutio speaks a little over two hundred and fifty lines of assorted prose and verse. With one remarkable exception his speeches are short, averaging less than four lines each; and with the same exception they handle only two themes: smut and fencing. So much has not often been made of smut and fencing; but these are rather trite materials out of which to construct the full character of a Renaissance princeling, and one may wonder whether Shakespeare would not have given Mercutio some other interests if he had been more at home with persons of his type. I think that the suspicion is strengthened when we look at Mercutio's one highly exceptional speech—the forty-one-line declamation that he so surprisingly devotes to Warwickshire folklore. As Pope might have said:

> The things, we know, are *amply* rich *and* rare,
> But wonder how the devil they got there.

The tone of this description of Mab, her equipage, and her pranks is beautifully Mercutian, but the theme is not a little strange and seems forcibly lugged in by Romeo's sudden remark: "I dream'd a dream to-night."

I will not take your time with arguments over the possibility that Mercutio's words about Mab *might* be later than *A Midsummer Night's Dream:* that they *might* show Shakespeare utilizing a residue of native folklore left on his hands after Mab was displaced by Titania and the Stratford fairies went classic. Shakespeare sometimes worked in this way; but it is much easier to believe that Mercutio's description— adhering so precisely to English village atmosphere and showing so much closer relationship to Drayton's *Nymphidia*—preceded *A Midsummer Night's Dream* and contains the germ of that play. It is unnecessary to labor this point, for surely a Shakespeare who knew his noblemen as Shakespeare shows that he knew Theseus in *A Midsummer Night's Dream* would not have needed to leave the social environment of his Capulet and Mercutio so incorrect and patchy.

We come finally to the Nurse's famous line, " 'Tis since the earthquake now eleven years," repeated a little later: "And since that time it is eleven years." Do we have to remember (as some commentators have urged us to do) that there was an earthquake in Ferrara in 1570? Or should we suppose (as others would have us) that the Nurse—always so proudly meticulous and so correct about statistics, from teeth to birthdays—was grossly misreckoning on this occasion?

There was only one earthquake that the English public of the 1590's would remember, and few would not remember the date of that: 1580. "The 6th of April," says Stowe, "being Wednesday in Easter week, about six of the clock towards evening, a sudden earthquake happening in London and almost generally throughout England, caused such amazedness of the people as was wonderful for that time, and caused them to make their earnest prayers unto Almighty God."

> Shake, quoth the dove-house. 'Twas no need, I trow,
> To bid me trudge:
> And since that time it is eleven years.

To me this sounds like an authentic experience. I rather fancy there was a real dove-house to shake, and a sixteen-year-old boy to observe and trudge, and later to incorporate his remembrance of the incident in a passage that gave a sense of lively contemporaneity to his play. If this is so, and Shakespeare was writing *Romeo and Juliet* in 1591, it is not surprising to find the tragedy still marked by evidences of social inexperience that would be hard to account for after 1594.

SHAKESPEARE'S DOVE-HOUSE

SOME years ago, when I was indulging my fancy concerning the possibly autobiographical quality of Shakespeare's talk about the earthquake and the dove-house in *Romeo and Juliet* I, iii ("Shakespeare Remembers his Youth in Stratford" in *Essays and Studies in Honor of Carleton Brown*, 1940), I was not aware that a very superior dove-house existed in 1580 and is still to be seen at Wilmcote, on or at least very close to the "Asbies" property which the poet's mother had inherited.

Mr. Oliver Baker's interesting book, *In Shakespeare's Warwickshire and the Unknown Years* (1937), reports the purchase, in 1929, and subsequent restoration by the Shakespeare Birthplace Trustees of "the very fine old house [at Wilmcote] which has been popularly known for many years as 'Mary Arden's Cottage,' an absurd name for what was not a cottage but a small manor-house. That it was a house of some importance is made clear by its size and the fine timbers that have been used in its construction, and also by the fact of its possessing a large stone pigeon-house" (p. 225). He goes on to say (p. 227):

An interesting feature of the Wilmcote farm is the ancient pigeon-house or dovecot. Shakespeare called them dove-houses. It has stone walls pierced with many nest-holes, which walls, as they were built only with local rubble, were, when bought by the Birthplace Trustees, bulging so much with age that it seemed dangerous to enter it. But Mr. William Weir, who is accustomed to repairing ancient and neglected buildings, said that he had saved many church towers that were much worse, and now after his treatment it is quite strong and likely to last for centuries.

"The pigeon-house at Wilmcote," Mr. Baker explains, is a rectangular edifice of limestone rubble, and was no doubt originally plastered. It has two gables of oak timbers, one facing the road and the other towards the farm. In the centre of the ridge is the usual louvre hole roofed over. The building measures twenty feet by seventeen externally, and inside is fifteen feet by twelve, so that walls are only two feet six inches thick, which may account for the dangerous state which it had reached when the Birthplace Trustees repaired it. . . . The presence of a large and ancient pigeon-house in the farmyard at Wilmcote is an interesting fact, as it seems to be evidence that the place was a manor-house; for nobody but a Lord of the Manor or a Rector was permitted to build one (p. 229).

This looks like unsolicited testimony in behalf of readers who get a sense of remembered incident rather than dramatic imagination out of this talk of "sitting in the sun under the dove-house wall" and "Shake, quoth the dove-house." Apparently we can without rebuke assume that the boy was indeed sitting there—on a visit to his step-grandmother, Agnes Arden, who died the following December—when the earthquake of the afternoon of April 6, 1580, occurred; and it may be that the earthquake started the disrepair in the dove-house which Mr. Baker and the Stratford Trustees have had to set right.

HAMLET'S THIRD SOLILOQUY

THE seven great soliloquies of Hamlet may be divided into two groups. Three of them—the first ("O, that this too too solid flesh would melt," etc., I.ii.129 ff.), the fourth ("To be or not to be," III.i. 56 ff.), and the sixth ("Now might I do it pat," etc., III. iii.73 ff.)—show the hero inert and overreflective, inclined to toy with the idea of suicide, to overlook the responsibilities of life, and speculate in an unhealthy manner on existence beyond the grave. Indeed, the fourth soliloquy—the famous "To be or not to be"—marks the lowest intellectual level reached by Hamlet. The complete selfishness of the argument, the refusal to recognize any duty to live for the sake of his mission, and the astonishing "bestial oblivion" evidenced by the allusion to

> The undiscover'd country from whose bourn
> No traveller returns

on the tongue of one who has recently spoken with his own father's ghost—these all shock the attentive reader and show the speaker's intelligence at its nadir. Such, I think, was clearly Shakespeare's intention; and despite the rhetorical brilliance of the lines when taken absolutely, the critic may well be pardoned a cynical amusement at the fact that just this speech and Polonius' fatuous advice to his son—advice very worthy of Lord Chesterfield—should be enshrined in the memory of the general public as particular gems of Shakespearian wisdom.

The three soliloquies just mentioned are all the product of a relatively quiescent frame of mind. The first is uttered before Hamlet has learned of his father's murder; the fourth is spoken in the quiet of the morning (?) before the play; while in the sixth, though the presence of Claudius disturbs Hamlet's conscience, the motionless and suppliant posture of the King evidently acts as a check on the speaker's emotions.

In the four other soliloquies we see Hamlet in far more normal and admirable moods, and each of these soliloquies is produced by a state of special excitement. The second immediately follows the exit of the Ghost, the third is inspired by the Player's moving declamation, the fifth follows the success of the "Mousetrap," and the seventh is evoked by the impressive sight of Fortinbras and his army. This last soliloquy is certainly the finest in the play, and it gives ground for the idea that Hamlet's tragedy arises not from the excessive postponement but from the too early development of the crisis. The fine words about the purposes of "god-like reason," the clear sense of personal power, the sympathetic appreciation of Fortinbras' spirit, coupled with the discriminating realization of what it is "Rightly to be great," evidence that "slight thinning of the dark cloud of melancholy" which Professor Bradley thinks he observes in the following (fifth) act.

Now this last soliloquy is a close and doubtless intentional counterpart of the third, which I wish more particularly to discuss. Both speeches mark a psychological progress from intense self-dissatisfaction and even self-abuse ("How all occasions do inform against me!"—"O, what a rogue and peasant slave am I!"), through elaborate self-analysis, to self-confidence; and each ends with an almost triumphant declaration of the speaker's practical resolution:

> O, from this time forth
> My thoughts be bloody, or be nothing worth!

> The play's the thing,
> Wherein I'll catch the conscience of the king.

In these two speeches, which represent a wider intellectual range than any other in the play, is to be found the surest key to Hamlet's mental difficulty; and the clue is most distinct in the earlier, which is the longer—indeed much the longest of all the soliloquies.

In the third soliloquy I find confirmation of Professor Bradley's theory of Hamlet's melancholy, of which that most careful critic seems inobservant. Indeed, it is strange to find that Professor Bradley and his most determined opponent, Mr. W. F. Trench, who thinks Hamlet definitely mad, occupy the same ground in their interpretation of the vastly important conclusion of the third soliloquy, where Hamlet resolves to test the King's guilt by means of the "Mousetrap."

Professor Bradley writes (*Shakespearean Tragedy*, p. 131): "Nothing, surely, can be clearer than the meaning of this famous soliloquy. [*Sic!*] The doubt which appears at its close, instead of being the natural conclusion of the preceding thoughts, is totally inconsistent with them. For Hamlet's self-reproaches, his curses on his enemy, and his perplexity about his own inaction, one and all imply his faith in the identity and truthfulness of the Ghost. *Evidently this sudden doubt, of which there has not been the slightest trace before, is no genuine doubt; it is an unconscious fiction, an excuse for his delay—and for its continuance.*"

Mr. Trench's explanation is essentially the same (*Shakespeare's Hamlet*, p. 126):

"The doubt upon this point [i.e. the King's guilt] is a supposititious doubt invented to excuse the substitution of another sort of action for the action that is required."

Now in the case of that other artist in soliloquies, Iago, we are accustomed to discount the probability of conscious or unconscious insincerity; but Hamlet is a very different character, and Shakespeare's dramatic problem is in his case altogether different. Iago's various insincerities mutually confute and explain one another and are explained by his many actions; but Hamlet does not thus interpret his words by the constant comment of action, and I can find no other instance in which his words seem intended to be taken at less than their full face value.

The idea, then, that Shakespeare ventured upon the hazardous expedient of requiring his auditors to understand the eloquent conclusion of this most elaborate soliloquy in a Pickwickian sense, as "no genuine doubt" or as "supposititious," would seem allowable only as a last resort after failure to discover any logical reason for the words. I cannot at all agree with Professor Bradley's assumption that the doubt about the King's guilt, "instead of being the natural conclusion of the preceding thoughts, is totally inconsistent with them." Let us consider the third soliloquy as a whole and in connection with the feelings which prompted it.

imagery

The speech is Hamlet's reaction on the Player's declamation concerning the death of Priam. In introducing that declamation, Shakespeare seems to have been actuated by three motives, of which the first two have been noted by the critics. I do not remember, however, to have seen any mention of the third and most important. Certainly it is ignored by Professor Bradley and Mr. Trench, whose difficulties regarding the following soliloquy can thus, I think, be accounted for.

The dramatic purposes of the "rugged Pyrrhus" declamation appear to be:

1. It continues the rather good-natured protest concerning the "little eyases" of the Queen's Chapel by an obvious though not very uncomplimentary parody of the turgid lines on the death of Priam in their play of *Dido* (by Marlowe and Nashe).

2. The Pyrrhus-Priam-Hecuba story furnishes a kind

of parallel to the Hamlet-Claudius-Gertrude story. As Mr. Trench well puts it: "Around the slaying of a king all Hamlet's thoughts ever revolve; so in this half-dramatized epic the most attractive passage of all is that about the death of Priam." (p. 104)

These are rather trivial and incidental purposes. By themselves they would hardly justify the intrusion of some seventy lines of melodramatic bombast, irrelevant to the actual story of Hamlet.

3. There is, however, an aspect in which the declamation has very decided relevance to Hamlet's case. Let us assume with Mr. Bradley that Shakespeare understands Hamlet to be suffering from melancholic depression, and then ask what effect upon his hero the dramatist would look for from such an exciting bit of dramatic entertainment. Clearly, a salutary effect. We all know how wonderfully fits of "blues" caused by disappointment or excessive introspection are alleviated by a play, particularly a wild farce or lurid melodrama. The mists of self absorption are cleared from our brains; we see our own troubles in proper focus and perspective.

So it is with Hamlet. It is no accident, I think, that the announcement of the players' coming finds him in the lowest spirits he has shown, complaining of his "bad dreams," confessing that "Denmark's a prison" and that man delights not him; no, nor woman neither. He brightens up at once when the actors are announced and becomes more normal and gayer in their presence. He thirsts for dramatic distraction. "We'll e'en to 't like French falconers," he cries; "we'll have a speech straight. . . . Come, a passionate speech." Perhaps the bad dramatic taste for which he is blamed in his praise of "Æneas's tale to Dido" is to be ascribed to his momentary craving for strong excitement. He listens avidly to the declamation and snubs Polonius savagely for finding it too long. When the en-

tertainment is over and Hamlet is left alone, the Aristo-
telian purgation by tragic pity and terror has been effected.
He is in the position of a mountain climber long held
inactive by befogging mist, when suddenly the cloud is
dispelled and instantaneously he sees his course before
him.

The great soliloquy which follows has two parts, quite
logically connected. In the first part, as the mists are blown
from his brain, Hamlet feels a natural wonder and disgust
that he has been inactive so long. The cause of delay, being
entirely psychological, is quite inconceivable when it is
momentarily removed. He contrasts himself with the actor
and proposes three hypothetical reasons for his failure to
perform the duty of vengeance: (1) he is "a dull and
muddy-mettled rascal"; (2) he is a coward; (3) he is an
ass that unpacks his heart with words. At this point he
contemptuously drops the vain search for causes, and like
the keen and efficient thinker he naturally is, turns his attention to the matter before him:

Fie upon't! foh! About, my brain!

In the second part of the soliloquy, Hamlet looks to the
future and apprehends no more difficulty than when the
vengeance was first asked of him. He sees nothing to stop
him. However, weeks have passed—perhaps two months
—since he heard the Ghost's words, and the impression of
the interview is inevitably less vivid than it was. The facts
of the revelation are perfectly clear, but naturally—how
could it be otherwise?—he no longer feels that ardent conviction of the trustworthiness of his supernatural visitant
which had enabled him to cry out to Horatio and Marcellus on the night of the meeting:

Touching this vision here,
It is an *honest* ghost, that let me tell you.

Hamlet now realizes what Horatio and Marcellus then realized—what the people of Shakespeare's time generally understood—that there are ghosts honest and ghosts dishonest. In the actual presence of the spirit he had no doubts, but could he conscientiously trust that feeling now? There is no effort to evade any responsibility or shield himself behind any supposititious or ungenuine doubt. He asks only what any scrupulous man must have demanded—"grounds more relative" than his two months' old recollection of his impression of the spirit's sincerity.

HAMLET is never more normal than at the end of this long and carefully prepared soliloquy. But the natural reaction follows. He sleeps the next night well, and when he awakes on the morning before the play the fog has again settled over his brain—the thicker doubtless for its temporary dispersal. The relapse after artificial relief such as has been offered to him is wont to be serious, and the "To be or not to be" soliloquy shows him indeed in the blankest despair. The performance of the play rouses him, but insufficiently. A dozen distractions press upon him. The speech beginning "'Tis now the very witching time of night" and still more that which commences "Now might I do it pat" show how uncertain of his course he is, and he ends by venting irresponsibly on Polonius the energy which in the third soliloquy he meant to direct against Claudius. Oblivion and fatalistic indifference follow. Then, as if to enforce the point of the third soliloquy, Shakespeare shows in the seventh how like causes produce like results in Hamlet's mind, when the cheap melodrama of Fortinbras' expedition again unclouds his brain and effects another brief moment of clear vision.

THE ROMANTIC IAGO

O F Shakespeare's characters," writes Professor Bradley, "Falstaff, Hamlet, Iago, and Cleopatra (I name them in the order of their births) are probably the most wonderful. Of these, again, Hamlet and Iago, whose births come nearest together, are perhaps the most subtle. And if Iago had been a person as attractive as Hamlet, as many thousands of pages might have been written about him, containing as much criticism good and bad."

Now heaven forfend that the mountainous cairn of commentary erected over the bones of him who so infelicitously remarked, "The rest is silence," be ever duplicated. But I am constrained to take up the cudgels against this general imputation of the unattractiveness of Iago and vindicate his place in the sun, beneath the beams of that romantic luminary which so irradiates all his great compeers: Honest Jack, the Prince of Denmark, and the Serpent of old Nile. We are prone to turn our scandalized backs upon Iago and flatter ourselves, as our ancestors have been doing since the days of Samuel Johnson, that the rogue shall never beguile us; and thus we miss the many evidences that Iago was to Shakespeare intensely, even romantically, attractive.

"Evil has nowhere else been portrayed with such mastery as in the character of Iago," Professor Bradley further remarks; and he goes on to declare: "It is only in Goethe's Mephistopheles that a fit companion for Iago can be found. Here there is something of the same deadly coldness, the same gaiety in destruction."

The gaiety in destruction we may admit—more easily

in Shakespeare's character perhaps than in Goethe's; but
the deadly Mephistophelian coldness of Iago requires
establishment. The difficulty is that what the critics see—
this chilly, almost passionless, egoism—is so remarkably at
variance with what Iago's companions in the play see in
him. (The qualities they all recognize are blunt honesty,
rough imperturbable good nature, extraordinary cordial-
ity and trustworthiness, hiding under the thinnest mask of
cynicism, as in real life they so often do.)

Shakespeare is at particular pains to emphasize the
unanimity and positiveness of this impression. At the beginning of the third act, by way of preliminary to the
great "temptation scene," he favors us with a regular sym-
posium on Iago's character. The witnesses are most varied
in experience, attitude of mind, and intimacy of acquaintance. Their evidence is overwhelmingly unanimous and
consistent. Says Cassio, the foppish Florentine: "I never
knew a Florentine more kind and honest." Says Emilia,
Iago's plain-spoken wife: "I warrant it [Cassio's misfor-
tune] grieves my husband, as if the case were his." Says
Desdemona: "O, that's an honest fellow!" Says Othello:
"This fellow's of exceeding honesty"; and much more to
the same effect.

The words are fully borne out in action. In their trust
of Iago all Iago's acquaintances are united. Roderigo lets
him have his purse as if the strings were his; Cassio accepts
his counsel unhesitatingly; Othello, searching his brain,
finds the idea of Iago's insincerity simply unbelievable;
Emilia, when finally confronted with irrefragable proof
of his duplicity, is thundersmitten, but still incredulous.
She turns in deepest indignation to Iago:

> Disprove this villain [Othello] if thou be'st a man:
> He says thou told'st him that his wife was false:
> I know thou did'st not, thou'rt not such a villain:
> Speak, for my heart is full.

It is Iago to whom Othello as a matter of course entrusts the safety of his bride on the voyage to Cyprus; it is he from whom Desdemona seeks such amelioration of distress as can be found during her anxiety lest Othello's ship has foundered; and it is Iago—not Gratiano, her uncle, or Lodovico—for whom she sends in her very darkest moment. "Prithee, to-night," she bids Emilia,

> Lay on my bed my wedding sheets: remember;
> And call thy husband hither.

It is Iago of whom she asks her most difficult question, "Am I that name, Iago?" and to whom she most turns for assistance:

> . . . O good Iago,
> What shall I do to win my lord again?
> Good friend, go to him.

Does Shakespeare then wish us to understand that this chilly egoist, this monster of "deadly coldness," has impressed a diametrically false conception of his nature upon his entire circle of acquaintance—upon the observant and the unobservant, upon men and women, upon the most intimate and the most casual associates alike? If so, the less Shakespeare he. Since the principle was so forcibly promulgated by Coleridge, it has been accepted as an axiom of criticism that Shakespeare never makes the claptrap device of surprise a main element in his plays. He does not much avail himself of its meretricious interest in the development of his plots; far less does he in the more essential matter of character. Lincoln's adage that you cannot fool all the people all the time is no more fully verified in life than in the plays of Shakespeare.

This honesty and innate kindliness of Iago, which all the characters in the play vouch for through practically the whole course of the action, can be no melodramatic villain's mask. A man of deadly coldness and natural selfishness does not thus impress his fellows. Shakespeare's plays, indeed, do present us with figures possessing something of the Mephistophelian coldness of heart predicated of Iago. Cassius in *Julius Caesar* has suggestions of it; Don John in *Much Ado* has a great deal more. Now what is the general opinion of these characters? Do we find the lean and hungry Cassius a common favorite? Do we find Don John universally trusted and appealed to as a man of exceeding honesty? Can we imagine Portia carrying her troubles to Cassius, or Hero selecting Don John for confidant, as Desdemona selects Iago?

It is evident, I think, that Shakespeare imagined Iago a man of warm sympathetic qualities, begetting confidence in his acquaintances as instinctively and universally as Don John's coldness begot distrust. Can we find in Shakespeare another character possessed of mental qualities like Iago's and exerting a similar influence upon his companions? There is one such, I think.

The adjective inevitably applied to Iago is "honest"; it is the regular epithet also of Falstaff. The coupling of Falstaff and Iago may seem bizarre, and their relation is indeed a kind of Jekyll-Hyde affair; but that Shakespeare saw a likeness seems capable of proof, and each throws welcome light upon the character of the other. We need not dwell long upon their more social aspects, since exigencies of plot, which multiplied scenes of jovial merrymaking almost to the point of fatty degeneration in the Falstaff plays, reduced to the minimum the treatment of the corresponding side of Iago. Yet it is clear that Iago, like Sir John, has heard the chimes at midnight and been merry twice and once. Only a seasoned habitué of the taverns could talk as he talks in the scene of the arrival at Cyprus and in the brawl scene, or sing as he sings:

> And let me the canakin clink, clink;
> And let me the canakin clink:
>   A soldier's a man;
>   Oh, man's life's but a span;
> Why, then, let a soldier drink.

In Iago's intellectual attitude we find reminiscences of Falstaff's way of thinking, just as we find reminiscences of Brutus in Hamlet. Falstaff's famous words on honor are virtually paraphrased in Iago's definition of reputation. "O, I have lost my reputation!" cries the disgraced Cassio. "I have lost the immortal part of myself!" "As I am an honest man," answers Iago, "I thought you had received some bodily wound; there is more sense in that than in reputation. Reputation is an idle and most false imposition, oft got without merit and lost without deserving: you have lost no reputation at all, unless you repute yourself such a loser."

One of Falstaff's most charming propensities is shared by Iago, and by no other character in Shakespeare. It is the trick of mischievously teasing the complaining victim, drawing him on from irritation to positive anger for sheer pride of intellectual superiority; allowing half-derisive confessions of abuse to accumulate till the victim is ready to strike, and then by a dexterous turn of phrase leaping clear away and leaving the dazed antagonist more firmly in his power than before. A good example is the passage in the second part of *Henry IV*, where Falstaff is caught slandering Prince Hal and Poins:

Falstaff. Didst thou hear me?
Prince. Yea, and you knew me, as you did when you ran away by Gadshill: you knew I was at your back, and spoke it on purpose to try my patience.
Falstaff. No, no, no; not so; I did not think thou wast within hearing.

Prince. I shall drive you then to confess the wilful abuse; and
    then I know how to handle you.
Falstaff. No abuse, Hal, on mine honor; no abuse.
Prince. Not to dispraise me, and call me pantler and bread-
    chipper and I know not what?
Falstaff. No abuse, Hal.
Poins. No abuse?
Falstaff. No abuse, Ned, in the world; honest Ned, none. I
    disprais'd him before the wicked, that the wicked might
    not fall in love with him.

Compare Iago, when the long-suffering Roderigo at
last turns upon him:

Roderigo. I do not find that thou deal'st justly with me.
Iago. What in the contrary?
Roderigo. Every day thou daff'st me with some device,
    Iago. . . . I will indeed no longer endure it, nor am I
    yet persuaded to put up in peace what already I have
    foolishly suffered.
Iago. Will you hear me, Roderigo?
Roderigo. Faith, I have heard too much, and your words and
    performances are no kin together.
Iago. You charge me most unjustly.
Roderigo. With nought but truth. . . .
Iago. Well; go to, very well.
Roderigo. Very well; go to! I cannot go to, man; nor 'tis not
    very well: nay, I think it is scurvy, and begin to find
    myself fopped in it.
Iago. Very well.
Roderigo. I tell you 'tis not very well. I will make myself
    known to Desdemona: if she will return me my jewels, I
    will give over my suit and repent my unlawful solicita-
    tion; if not, assure yourself I will seek satisfaction of you.
Iago. You have said now.
Roderigo. Ay, and said nothing but what I protest intend-
    ment of doing.

Iago. Why, now I see there's mettle in thee, and even from
this instant do build on thee a better opinion than ever
before.

Falstaff and Iago are indeed Shakespeare's two great
studies in materialism. Mentally and morally, they are
counterparts. That they affect us so differently is due to
the difference between the comic and the tragic environment. Still more it is due to difference in age. Falstaff, with
his load of years and flesh, is a static force. Taking his ease
at his inn, he uses his caustic materialistic creed and his
mastery of moral paradox but as a shield to turn aside the
attacks of a more spiritual society. Iago has looked upon
the world for only four times seven years. His philosophy
is dynamic. It drives him to assume the offensive, to take
up arms against what he thinks the stupidity of a too little
self-loving world. The flame, which in Falstaff only warms
and brightens, sears in Iago; but it is much the same kind
of flame and it attracts the same kind of moths. One may
even imagine with a mischievous glee the warping and
charring of green wit which would have resulted if Prince
Hal and Poins had fluttered about Falstaff when he too
was twenty-eight and "not an eagle's talon in the waist."

Iago is no more a born devil than Falstaff. He too might
have gone merrily on drinking and singing, consuming the
substance of two generations of Roderigos, till he too
waxed fat and inert and unequivocally comic. His diab-
olism is an accident, thrust upon him early in the play,
when in seeking to convince Roderigo of his hate for
Othello he convinces himself likewise, and suddenly finds
himself over head and ears in the depths of his own egoism, vaguely conscious that he is being used for the devil's
purposes but incapable either of shaping the direction or
checking the progress of his drift. There is, indeed, something suggestive of demoniacal possession in the way Iago
yields during the first two acts to influences which he

recognizes as diabolical but cannot at all understand. He whispers:

> I have 't. It is engender'd. Hell and Night
> Must bring this monstrous birth to the world's light;

and again:

> . . . 'Tis here, but yet confus'd:
> Knavery's plain face is never seen till us'd.

What he should say is not "I have 't," but "It has me." Shakespeare is peculiarly careful to exclude the possibility of anything like cold calculation or preconception of purpose.

Iago's ruin results from two by-products of his Falstaffian materialism. In the first place, the materialistic theory of life corrodes the imagination. In Iago's case, as in Falstaff's, it cuts its victim off from his future and ultimately severs his bond of sympathy with his fellows. It leaves him only the sorry garden patch of present personal sensation. There, indeed, the will can fitfully play the gardener, as Iago boasts, "plant nettles, or sow lettuce, set hyssop and weed up thyme, supply it with one gender of herbs, or distract it with many"; but it cannot range with large discourse or labor serenely toward a future harvest.

A natural corollary is that the materialist makes large and ever larger demands upon the present. Like the clown in Marlowe's *Faustus*, when he buys his shoulder of mutton so dear, he "had need have it well roasted and good sauce to it." Ennui grows constantly more unendurable and more unavoidable. Falstaff's life is a series of desperate escapes from boredom; it is for this that he joins the Gadshill party, that he volunteers for the wars. It is for this that he so carefully husbands Shallow: "I will devise matter enough out of this Shallow to keep Prince Harry in continual laughter the wearing out of six fashions." And Falstaff thinks with rueful envy of the capacity of romantic youth for sensation: "O, it is much that a lie with a slight oath and a jest with a sad brow will do with a fellow that never had the ache in his shoulders!"

It is for this that Iago so carefully secures Roderigo and his well-filled purse to spice his life in Cyprus. To avoid tedium is the great purpose of his existence, and truly his efforts are heroic. The brawl scene, with all its sinister potentialities, is for him a triumphant campaign against the blues. When at the close of the second act he looks up into the coming dawn and reviews the doings of the night, he is simply grateful for the anodyne he has ministered to himself. "By the mass," he exclaims, " 'tis morning. Pleasure and action make the hours seem short." Be the future what it may, five hours have been saved from dullness!

Of course, Iago clings to a plot which offers such relief. Of course, his narcotized sensibilities prevent him from understanding the exquisite poignancy of others' feelings. Jealousy, we gather, is for him a welcome, though nearly exhausted, source of distraction, offering him the alleviation a man with toothache may get when he bites his finger. How should he know Othello? And so he allows his dread of inactivity, his incorrigible craving for sensation, to drive him on through the temptation scene and all its, to him, fantastic consequences. His plot succeeds so well because he really has no plot. He dances from one mischievous suggestion to another with the agility and unsearchable purposefulness of a sleepwalker.

For Shakespeare, and the Elizabethans, less touchy than we about the particular ideals he shatters, I think Iago was distinctly attractive. Never, probably, was he more delightful to his companions than while his wild scheme spins through his irresponsible brain. Never, doubtless, did he more impress them with his "honesty," his lively, capable, warmhearted geniality. His spirit is fired with "pleasure and action," and he is almost lightheaded. His case is just the converse of Hamlet's. In one play we have the problem of the exhilarated materialist, in the other the problem of the soured idealist.

Shakespeare is a great believer in the school of experience, and his tragedies commonly teach the lessons of that school. Lear is a notable instance; Iago is another. His crusted materialism fails to stand the test of actual practice to which he puts it. Pitted against the idealism of those whom Iago thinks fools, it is first pierced and then broken. When he makes his speech about reputation in the second act, he is no doubt quite honest; the contrary feeling of Cassio awakes his genuine surprise and irritation. But Cassio's is evidently a real feeling and one that challenges consideration. The next morning he paraphrases the idealistic conception:

> Good name in man, and woman, dear my lord,
> Is the immediate jewel of their souls.

He employs the sentiment, of course, for his own purposes, and perhaps with inward derision, but the day before, he would hardly have believed it could exist in reasonable men. To express the idea at all throws open a window of the soul. Another window is opened when his wife unwittingly presents him with his moral photograph:

> I will be hang'd, if some eternal villain,
> Some busy and insinuating rogue,
> Some cogging, cozening slave, to get some office,
> Have not devis'd this slander; I'll be hang'd else.

Suddenly he sees himself in the new spiritual light which things are taking on, and he recoils incredulous:

> Fie, there is no such man; it is impossible.

Last scene of all, we hear Iago in his final soliloquy, hedged about by the desperate perils which his own moral obtuseness has drawn upon him. Only by homicide of the wildest sort can he hope to escape, but he reasons, with a weary detachment, of his chances, and he offers as a chief inducement to the reckless game the new motive of shame:

> . . . If Cassio do remain,
> He hath a daily beauty in his life
> That makes me ugly.

Even the "counter-caster," Cassio, whose one admirable trait is his selfless hero worship of Othello, now seems clothed in a beauty of character which makes the materialist hate himself and drives him to desperate courses. How impossible such an attitude would be to the scornful Iago of the first acts! We have thus a measure of the moral awakening of Iago. His very crimes lead him to a purer sense of the values of life. As elsewhere—in *Lear, Macbeth, Hamlet, Julius Caesar*—the poet's doctrine is that false principles, if left free play, will undo themselves and work their own refutation.

We need a spectroscope for Shakespeare. Our perception of Iago is blurred by the glow of sympathy we feel for Othello and for Desdemona. But in so far as we can eliminate these two luminous figures from our view, we can see the outlines of what I fancy was the poet's original idea, the tragedy of Iago, the tragedy of the honest, charming soldier, who swallowed the devil's bait of self-indulgence, grew blind to ideal beauty, and in his blindness overthrew more than his enemies.

> . . . What is a man,
> If his chief good and market of his time
> Be but to sleep and feed? A beast, no more.

Iago illustrates Hamlet's words. So, less luridly, does Falstaff, and the parallel may explain the poet's alleged harshness in the rejection of Falstaff by his king. But Falstaff's creator, as he brought Iago to a realization of Cassio's "daily beauty," gave Sir John also at his death a glimpse of the ideal: "A' babbled of green fields."

KING LEAR ON THE STAGE

WHY is it that *King Lear*, perhaps the most passionate, the noblest, and even the most personal of Shakespeare's works, is, by the verdict of criticism and theatrical experience alike, a poor stage play? This is a question which has received no adequate answer. Yet on the answer to it depends in large measure our decision concerning the mature Shakespeare's attitude toward life and art. Is it, as Swinburne asserts, because *Lear* represents a world of unmitigated blackness, lightened only by the lurid flames of terrible passion or hideous impiety? Is it, as Charles Lamb believed, that the figures in *Lear* are too grand, the emotions too intense and exalted, for visual presentation? Or must we conclude with Professor Bradley that *Lear* is different in its essence from Shakespeare's other tragedies: that it is really a dramatic poem, destined for the study rather than the stage, and intrinsically incapable of acting?

It seems possible to give a decided negative to all these queries, while fully recognizing the peculiar quality in the play which they attempt to explain. The careful study of *King Lear* necessitates no reversal of judgment concerning Shakespeare's relation to the world. Nowhere does the poet point more forcibly the true dramatic moral that "It's wiser being good than bad," that good is its own reward and evil its own punishment. Nor is more than a very dangerous half-truth contained in the criticism which takes *King Lear* as a play apart, a voicing of lyric or philosophic rather than dramatic ideas, a special unveiling of the poet's darkest privacies, to be analyzed like *Samson Agonistes* or the second part of *Faust*, but never, even in thought, to be staged.

Of course *King Lear* leaves on the casual reader a deep impression of gloom. It seems to be in an unusual degree a "personal" work; and it appears never to have lent itself so easily to theatrical presentation as the other great tragedies of Shakespeare. Yet we know that this play was written, like the rest, for acting, and that it was acted, as the Stationers' Register tells us, "before the king's majesty at Whitehall upon St. Stephen's night at Christmas [Dec. 26, 1606] by his majesty's servants playing usually at the Globe on the Bankside." Study of *King Lear*, moreover, brings out nothing more clearly than the essential unity of Shakespeare's attitude to life, thus setting right the mischievous perversion which would make of the poet's career a kind of April day, a thing of moods and changes, each self-sufficient and thoughtless of the rest—beginning with the gay sunshine of the morning period and extending, through showers, into the blackness of thunder, and then into a dewy serenity of eve, a dramatic fools' paradise of universal reconciliation which takes no heed of the storms passed by but elsewhere raging.

The cause of *King Lear's* relative failure to appeal on our stage is that Shakespeare stands here at odds, not with himself, but with the conventional tragic standards and with the general public's estimate of life. The play suffers, not from excessive grandeur, but, on the contrary, because its most significant situations manifest to us, when visually presented, something less than tragic proportions. *Lear* is one of the boldest examples of the "bürgerliches Trauerspiel," a type always ungrateful to the snobbery of audiences and the conservatism of tragic tradition.

From the time of Aristotle, public opinion has expected of tragedy that it be "an imitation of a worthy or illustrious action, possessing magnitude"; that its main figures be in station or talent, if not in righteousness, the salt of the earth, and that it deign to rest its exalted catastrophe on none but the more stately passions; on those, for instance, which issue in murder or treason, incest or adultery. Many writers have, indeed, protested, like Grillparzer and Ibsen, or like the nameless authors of Elizabethan domestic tragedies, against the more formal part of this demand, and they have made good their right to fit bourgeois characters to aristocratic themes and emotions. In *King Lear* Shakespeare has taken a bolder step. Not only has he chosen to present under the tattered veil of mythical royalty a bourgeois family group; he has even dethroned all the conventional tragic passions and elevated to the highest place in the whole hierarchy of sin his detested petty vice of selfishness. In this play—to the bewilderment of reader or spectator, but in fullest accord with Shakespeare's final verdict on life—we find the usual concomitants of loftiest tragedy attending as mean and scarce considered handmaids on the central theme of filial undutifulness. In recalling the play we pass almost inattentively the incidents of murder, suicide, adultery, treason, civil discord, war, and torture, to weep over the wounded vanity of a silly old man or shudder at his exposure in a casual storm.

Not till our modern life grows less prolific of unsisterly and undaughterly types, till squabbling and jealous self-seeking cease to be for us facts of universal acceptance and become hideous monstrosities, will it be easy for the spectator to grasp the true moral of *King Lear*. One of the healthiest features of Shakespeare's work is the honest disgust which sordid egoism inspires in him always. In so early and happy a play even as *As You Like It*, "man's ingratitude" appears to him the unkindest and keenest of human ills; and the same loathing deepens as his experience grows broader, till it finds expression in the almost unmixed vileness of Cloten, Caliban, and the other mean figures which go so far to disprove the idea that Shakespeare's last plays preach a spirit of truce and reconciliation with the hateful things of life.

In *King Lear* Shakespeare has attempted, at the darkest period apparently of his career, a tragedy after his own heart, a tragedy of those less erected vices which assuredly the poet believed more loathsome and more ruinous than all the spectacular sins and passions usually treated. The first scene of *King Lear* introduces us to a family party: a selfish old man, whom royal estate has not dignified and age has not made wise, and three inharmonious daughters —two grasping, vulgar, and hypocritical, the third good with a rigid and almost chilling virtue. The poet's purpose is to show that the tragedy of mortal existence grows quite as freely out of such ordinary types and situations as from more abnormal causes. The foundations of this gigantic drama are all matters generally regarded as commonplace —events which would hardly have attracted the notice of an Elizabethan balladmonger or a modern journalist.

Evidently, such a subject, however it might appear to Shakespeare, would not be accepted as tragic by the groundlings either of his day or our own. Here seems to lie the main difficulty of the play: what Shakespeare conceives to be the essence of tragedy is for the average audience either a trite commonplace of daily life or mere matter for humorous diversion. To give the semblance of tragedy to such a theme, the poet has been driven to an artificial heightening of his effects. To enforce his moral of the beastliness of selfish humanity, he has borrowed from Sidney's *Arcadia* the gruesome story of the blinding of Gloster. Furthermore, in the last two acts, which yet constitute the least affecting part of the play, he has piled high the conventional horrors. The result is both a triumph and a failure. The dullest spectator is indeed cudgeled into seeing that here tragic issues are afoot; but neither he nor the casual reader is likely to see the tragedy where Shakespeare seems to see it clearest: in the self-justifying and speciously reasonable egoism of Goneril and Regan during the first three acts, an egoism which may develop into the open villainy of the final acts, but which is infinitely more dangerous and despicable in its less advanced form.

"Let them anatomize Regan; see what breeds about her heart. Is there any cause in nature that makes these hard hearts?" In these words of Lear we have surely the kernel of the drama—the baffling question of the reason for human inhumanity, the most persistent, apparently, of all the problems which Shakespeare's life experience set his imagination to solve. In *King Lear* the poet has undertaken, if not to read the riddle, at least to state definitely its terms.

There are three pivotal characters in the play: Goneril, Regan, and Lear; and we may regard the work from two points of view. We may consider it roughly as a whole, with particular attention to the last acts, and call it, as Professor Bradley suggests, "The Redemption of King Lear," the optimistic story of an old man's rescue through suffering from a life of intolerant selfishness. Or we may look more particularly at the first half of the drama and call it "The Case of Goneril and Regan." It is this latter aspect, doubtless, which first attracted the poet, and which seems responsible for nearly all the play's difficulties.

Goneril and Regan are always thought monsters of evil, and so they indubitably appeared to Shakespeare. Yet the spectator who watches them through the first two acts and a half may find it difficult to justify his detestation. Till the beginning of the storm scenes in Act III, worldly reason would even pronounce in favor of the two daughters as opposed to their domineering and vindictive father. The dramatist's purpose, indeed, is to dethrone just this cold reason of the law court, which freezes the sympathies and apotheosizes self-interest; and no human being can remain dispassionate before Lear's mighty imprecations. Subconsciously, however, any spectator and almost any reader must probably feel with bewilderment the conflict of two standards of judgment: that by which he, as a member of the callous world, condones the uncharity of two mean-spirited but as yet unsinning daughters; and that other standard which, when expressed in the illogical and frantic curses of Lear, withers and makes ugly the snug complacency of worldly wisdom.

Up to the end of Act II, when Lear, scorning the offer of shelter "for his particular," rushes headlong from Gloster's house to tear his passion to tatters amid the accompaniment of wind, rain, desolation, and the most lurid adventitious heightenings ever devised by poet to elevate senile impatience to the level of tragedy—up to this point there is little doubt that in actual life philistine common sense would side with Goneril and Regan. Even while carried with Lear on the full tide of indignation, the reader can hardly escape the half sense of his own hypocrisy in condemning so heartily the figures on the stage, while lightly forgiving their counterparts of his acquaintance who are likewise given inches and who take ells in the subordination of their elders and the ordering of their households according to their proper satisfaction. Certainly the short patience of Goneril and Regan must have been severely tried. Kent and Cordelia found Lear's undisputed authority hard to bear; and the task of adjusting his wayward will to another's rule must have been many times more difficult.

> How in one house
> Should many people under two commands
> Hold amity? (II, iv, 243 ff.)

Truly, when the one command is Lear's and the other Regan's, the question finds no answer.

For Lear the head and front of Goneril's offending is her effort to reduce the number of his retainers. This is, of course, a breach of contract, and if submissively endured might prove but a beginning for other petty indignities. Yet we must admit that there is good show of justice in the daughter's complaint:

> Your insolent retinue
> Do hourly carp and quarrel, breaking forth
> In rank and not-to-be-endured riots. (I, iv, 221 ff.)

Lear's followers can certainly not have conduced to the quiet of a royal establishment; and the ordinary worldling may feel something of Goneril's impatience against the

> Idle old man,
> That still would manage those authorities
> That he hath given away,

against the self-deposed king, who would shuffle off the pains and responsibilities of monarchy and yet retain the power of making himself with his hundred henchmen a sort of lord of misrule in his daughter's dominion. Of course, the apology for this, as for Lear's other faults, is old age; but this very age which deepens our reverence and pity for the father also excuses to some extent the daughters' attempt to curtail his freedom.

In portraying the relations between the members of this family, tragedy appears to be trespassing on the pre-scriptive domain of comedy, and is sometimes able to make good its position only by a rather artificial appeal to the emotions. Thus the terrible and beautiful storm scenes in Act III would seem to the coldly logical spectator a dra-matic inconsequence, if any spectator could conceivably remain logical under this hurricano of emotion. How does it concern the question of tragic responsibility that the night into which Lear rushes—of his own motion, we should remember—is stormy rather than clear? Yet this storm is the mainspring of the play. It is probably the best remembered incident in the drama. It is, with the lurid jesting of the fool and the raving of Edgar, the blast furnace that raises the smouldering flames of domestic discord to the white heat of tragedy. Try to imagine a storm which could make itself heard amid the mental tumult of the third act of *Othello*, and you have a measure of the difference in tension between the two works. In *Othello* and *Macbeth*, the poet has only to guide and keep within decorous limits the flying career of genuinely tragic incident; in *King Lear* we may see him driving with loosened reins, lashing into the swiftness and energy of true tragedy of the duller progress of life's commonplace.

Of course, Shakespeare succeeds, and so transcendently that *Lear* arouses deeper and more painful emotions than any of those plays where the tragic matter lay clearer at hand. Yet it is not impossible to detect signs here and there that the tragic mood is being forced. Lear's imprecations upon his daughters can hardly justify themselves before the spectator who forms his opinion entirely by what he sees on the stage. It is very doubtful whether they can be justified at all, except as personal attacks of the poet against that ogre of self-love which the world of his day and of ours refuses to disown. Hardly even the old king's savage words to Cordelia in the first scene are more disproportioned to the offense than is his curse of Goneril in scene iv:

> Hear, Nature hear! dear goddess, hear!
> Suspend thy purpose, if thou didst intend
> To make this creature fruitful, etc. (I, iv, 297 ff.)

It is no wonder if, after this truly awful execration, straight from the heart of the poet, the spectator feels that in Goneril all the evil of the world is embodied; but it would be strange if he should not feel vaguely a doubt as to just where this evil has outwardly expressed itself. We must all be somewhat inclined to repeat Albany's bewildered question, "Now, gods that we adore, whereof comes this?" Of no single action, truly; but because she, who to the average one of us might appear not too unlike ourselves, is to Lear, seeing with the poet's eyes, the image of all that is most mean and abhorrent in life.

Far as we may be led in condemnation of Lear's elder daughters, we cannot reasonably approve their father's attitude toward them. It is, indeed, only more just than his treatment of Cordelia in that the darts which the old man's injured vanity sends blindly forth happen in the one case to strike the guilty, while in the other they fall not much more lightly or with much less provocation upon the innocent. What distortion of justice is involved in his words of Goneril!

> She hath abated me of half my train;
> Look'd black upon me; struck me with her tongue,
> Most serpent-like, upon the very heart.
> All the stor'd vengeances of heaven fall
> On her ingrateful top! Strike her young bones,
> You taking airs, with lameness! (II, iv, 161 ff.)

Regan's answer, "So will you wish on me, When the rash mood is on," may be prompted as much by reason as by the consciousness of ill deserving.

Sometimes Shakespeare's desire to arouse sympathy with the injured father does not prevent him from treating Lear's foolish petulance with open irony; as when the misguided man promises himself that his "kind and comfortable" second daughter shall with her nails flay the "wolvish visage" of the elder (I, iv, 329 ff.); or when, at the very end of the second act, we find him still so untutored by adversity as to repeat and parody the foolish

love test with which his tragedy began, still playing the
one daughter against the other, haggling over the number
of his retainers, and mean enough still to turn to the hated
and abused Goneril with these words of ineffable weakness:

> I'll go with thee:
> Thy fifty yet doth double five-and-twenty,
> And thou art twice her love. (II, iv, 261 ff.)

Throughout the first half of the play Lear is totally
wrongheaded. As Shakespeare's spokesman he scourges
the selfishness of the world, but he deserves and receives
an equal scourge for his own. What is his finest speech in
Act II but a piece of glorious special pleading, an illegiti-
mate appeal to the emotions, which fails to touch the real
issues?

> You see me here, you gods, a poor old man,
> As full of grief as age; wretched in both!
> If it be you that stir these daughters' hearts
> Against their father, fool me not so much
> To bear it tamely; touch me with noble anger,
> And let not woman's weapons, water-drops,
> Stain my man's cheeks! (II, iv, 275 ff.)

Nor is there real justice in Lear's ravings in the most
exalted scene of the play, where he stands in the storm,
surrounded and comforted by the truest followers that
man could have, and rails against humanity:

> And thou, all-shaking thunder,
> Strike flat the thick rotundity o' the world!
> Crack nature's moulds, all germens spill at once
> That make ingrateful man! (III, ii, 6 ff.)

The violence of this universal malediction, uttered thus
in the Timon vein, tenses the nerves and quickens the emotions of the auditors; but that the poet ever meant it to be

taken as a just indictment of the world which contains Kent and Cordelia, the Fool, Edgar, and Gloster, is, of course, unbelievable. The true moral of the play is spoken, not by Lear in any of his diatribes, but by the least admirable of all the characters, by Regan herself, when she says:

> O, sir, to wilful men,
> The injuries that they themselves procure
> Must be their schoolmasters. (II, iv, 305 ff.)

Viewed in its widest significance, the drama is a record of the schooling of Lear's self-love, a record of his cleansing through passion and suffering from the mire of egoism in which he, as well as his two daughters, has been steeped. For the spectator who could see thus far beneath the superficial worldliness and haphazard of the tragedy into the spirit that informs it, all discrepancies would vanish and the chaos of meanness give place to a universe where good is ordered from above, where selfishness and malice become the agents of chastisement and regeneracy. The wrong that Lear does and the wrong that he suffers are both productive in the end of benefit. Even the apparently fatal and inexcusable folly of Lear's conduct to Cordelia becomes an instrument of good to both. For the Cordelia of the last two acts is a much wiser and nobler character than the self-righteous girl who is so forward at the beginning to defy parental authority and convict parental unwisdom. To Lear himself the break with Cordelia becomes the first unwitting step in the way of salvation, for the accomplishment of his original purpose to make his abode with his youngest daughter can hardly have resulted happily for either his character or his fortunes. Even though we imagine Cordelia many times more angel than the first act shows her, must we not see in Lear's relations with her a prospect of bickerings and disputes leading at length to the old king's angry withdrawal to the jealous elder sisters and a sequel of total alienation, civil war, and ruin?

As it is, the story of Lear's sufferings is the story of his redemption. The first sign of unselfishness which he displays appears when he checks his anger against Cornwall:

> Tell the hot duke that—
> No, but not yet; may be he is not well:
> Infirmity doth still neglect all office
> Whereto our health is bound; we are not ourselves
> To suffer with the body. I'll forbear;
> And am fallen out with my more headier will,
> To take the indispos'd and sickly fit
> For the sound man. (II, iv, 105 ff.)

Generosity shows itself more strongly in the storm scenes in Lear's occasional touches of tender feeling for his followers, and it suddenly bursts over his clouded spirit with the force of a great new discovery in the quick flash of sympathy for the unknown poor:

> Poor naked wretches, wheresoe'er you are,
> That bide the pelting of this pitiless storm,
> How shall your houseless heads and unfed sides,
> Your loop'd and window'd raggedness, defend you
> From seasons such as these? O! I have ta'en
> Too little care of this. (III, iv, 28 ff.)

From this point there can be no question of our love for Lear. Our interest in his fate increases through the pathos of the wonderful scene of reconciliation with Cordelia to the august end, where the king has achieved his soul and where the bitter anguish of his last moments adds to his death something of the grace and even the joy of martyrdom.

In spite, then, of its black pictures of meanness and hypocrisy—or even because of these—*King Lear* is a play of good cheer, a powerful witness to the presence and potency in this world of faith, hope, and charity. Only very superficially does it seem to contradict Shakespeare's normal view of life; in reality it is pervaded by the kind of optimism which is most truly characteristic of him— not, of course, the shallow complacency which would close its eyes to the presence of evil, lulling itself with the siren's motto, "Whatever is, is right," but the strong faith that fiercely and confidently attacks evil where it sees it, knowing that the conflict can produce only greater and purer good.

Throughout this tragedy, so often called a work of darkness and despair, Shakespeare has preached with an emphasis almost melodramatic the necessary failure of wickedness. We have the proposition stated once in the conversation of the two servants after Gloster's blinding:

Sec. Serv. I'll never care what wickedness I do,
      If this man [Cornwall] come to good.
Third Serv.   If she live long,
      And in the end meet the old course of death,
      Women will all turn monsters. (III, vii, 99 ff.)

And pat comes the answer; for Cornwall has his death already upon him, and Regan lives only to die more shamefully in her moment of success. As if to impress the point, Albany repeats the same idea:

> If that the heavens do not their visible spirits
> Send quickly down to tame these vile offences,
> It will come,
> Humanity must perforce prey on itself,
> Like monsters of the deep. (IV, ii, 46 ff.)

And a few lines later, on hearing the news of Cornwall's death, he can say:

> This shows you are above,
> You justicers, that these our nether crimes
> So speedily can venge! (IV, ii, 78 ff.)

The end of the play clinches the moral. Evil has consumed itself and vanished like the shadowy negation that it is, while righteousness, purer and nobler for the late struggle, triumphs in the bright memories of Cordelia and Lear and in the living figures of Kent, Edgar, and Albany. This, surely, is the purest optimism and the truest philosophy. But it is a philosophy which can reveal itself on the stage only to the spectator capable of reading behind the superficial hyperboles of tragic usage a particularly simple and universal story of everyday humanity.

SHAKESPEARE'S STUDY IN CULTURE AND ANARCHY

THE stones which the Victorian builders rejected are in this later age become the cornerstones of new Shakespearean temples. Since the war we appear to have notably less to say about the serene and tranquil comedies (let it be hoped we do not read them less!) and our critics have been manifesting over a still longer period a disinclination to fling their caps for those idols of the age of Dowden, the honorable and self-satisfied Brutus and the efficient Henry V. Instead one finds one's friends discovering strange beauties in the torsos of Shakespeare's gallery, in the cryptic and provocative works which the Victorians damned with the epithet of "bitter." Thus *Measure for Measure, Timon of Athens,* and even *All's Well that Ends Well* awake a livelier interest than *As You Like It* now can stir. Half a dozen years ago Mrs. A. Y. Campbell wrote for *The London Mercury* a spirited, if too "timely," justification of *Troilus and Cressida* as a play *par excellence* of postwar disillusionment, a work of "bitter realism, a painfully exact drawing of the most wretched features of war," in which "the middle foreground is filled with those vain, noisy, godforsaken rowdies whom Shakespeare has labelled Achilles, Ajax, Diomed, Paris, Patroclus, and so forth." In this country, Professor Tatlock has devoted to the same once discredited play, in which he sees "the chief problem in Shakespeare," some of the most incisive and satisfying scholarship that we have lately had.

This means, of course, that our age, like other ages, looks for something of itself in Shakespeare, and naturally finds it. It is, I believe, a fact that the broken lights of our recent thinking have been playing remarkably around the edges of Shakespeare's work, and that certain new peripheral peaks stand out like mountains in the moon, with a perhaps deceptive but imposing clearness. And so, before the age of pure reason returns and these apparent glimpses behind the exposed surface of Shakespeare's mind grow indiscernible to a centrally focused criticism, let us set down some of the things we seem to see. Doubtless it should be done, as in this essay is intended, without dogmatism and without consciously incorporating the views of other observers.

That colossal and magnificent failure, *Troilus and Cressida*, I should like to present as one of Shakespeare's subtlest studies of the effect of environment on character and as his most definite realization of the social forces operative in England at the end of Queen Elizabeth's reign. Three strands of source material make up its fabric, and the first of these, in importance as in sequence, is Chaucer.

Had Shakespeare, as many have said, read his predecessor's great poem inattentively, or with prejudice and dislike? If so, the less Shakespeare he. But to dispel the notion we need surely do no more than ourselves read the sublime and touching stanzas in Chaucer's fifth book that describe the heartsick tryst of Troilus upon Troy wall:

> The day go'th faste, and after that com eve,
> And yit com nought to Troilus Criseyde.
> He loketh forth by hegge, by tree, by greve,
> And fer his hed over the wal he leyde;
> And at the laste he torned him and seyde,
> "By God, I wot her mening now, Pandare!
> Almost, y-wis, al newe was my care! . . .
> I wot she meneth riden prively. . . .
> By night into the town she thenketh ride,
> And, dere brother, thenk not long t'abide."

Let us read this and then recall the indisputable evidence that Shakespeare has been there before us, setting a perpetual note of admiration against these stanzas by the words with which he opens the last act of *The Merchant of Venice:*

> The moon shines bright: in such a night as this,
> When the sweet wind did gently kiss the trees
> And they did make no noise, in such a night
> Troilus methinks mounted the Troyan walls
> And sigh'd his soul toward the Grecian tents,
> Where Cressid lay that night.

We must not believe that he who wrote these words failed to realize what Chaucer was driving at, or ever forgot his Chaucer. We must not, I think, if we would interpret Shakespeare's play aright, doubt that it bears the proper title—that it is fundamentally the play of Chaucer's defeated lovers, a frailer Romeo and Juliet, "whose misadventur'd piteous overthrows" could not be romantically glorified as a moral victory, and perhaps for just that reason made special appeal to a dramatist who, by the period of *Hamlet* and *Troilus and Cressida,* had lost his joy in successful people.

I cannot believe that Shakespeare shared the contempt which the Elizabethan public generally and the race of modern critics have felt for Cressida. She is a more helpless being than Chaucer's Criseyde, a flower growing in Trojan slime, a little soiled from the first and shrinkingly conscious of her predestined pollution; yet Shakespeare's attitude to her is much more that of Chaucer than that of Ulysses, or of Sir Sidney Lee. In her relations with both her lovers he shows us the pathos of a daintiness reaching vainly after nobility, a wistful sincerity which knows it lacks strength to be the thing it would be. "Sweet, bid me hold my tongue," says she to Troilus in her most candid and assured moment—

> For in this rapture I shall surely speak
> The thing I shall repent;

and to Diomed in her last scene, with hardly less candor and simplicity,

> Sweet honey Greek, tempt me no more to folly.

Ancient Pistol may gibe at "the lazar kite of Cressid's kind," and the cold Ulysses cry, "Fie, fie, upon her!" But Shakespeare does not cry "Fie!" Rather, I think, we hear him whisper, "But yet the pity of it, Ulysses! O Ulysses, the pity of it!"

When Shakespeare came—it was probably in 1602, while the Elizabethan age was sluggishly ebbing into the Jacobean—to realize in a play this Chaucerian story of frosted romance, he had recourse to two further books, which he used to create an outward world for Troilus and Cressida. Since 1596 he might have known the Elizabethan version of Caxton's Troy book, *The Ancient History of the Destruction of Troy*, "newly corrected by W. Fiston." (He can hardly have known the previous editions, of which the last had been printed as far back as 1553.) Since 1598 he can have known the earliest and only relevant installments of Chapman's Homer. Both these bizarrely opposite reconstructions of life at Troy he certainly did know when he wrote his play; and to understand the nature of that play I think it is not necessary to assume that he knew much else, except of course always Chaucer.

Now the two salient features of the Caxton account (translated from Lefèvre's fifteenth-century French) are: first, that it concentrates attention strongly upon the people within the walls of Troy, the Trojans; and, second, that it narrates the incidents of the siege in exaggeratedly medieval, chivalresque manner after the fashion of Malory

or Froissart. Armored knights on horseback fight san-
guinary battles that are described like tournaments, and
bring their copious wounds to scars during long truces of
six months each. It is not true that Caxton (or Lefèvre)
shows any moral preference for the Trojan side. On the
contrary, he makes it far clearer than Homer does that the
Trojans are in the wrong: that their policy is vindictive
and treacherous, that Priam is thoroughly dishonest, and
Paris a dastardly sensualist and assassin. Hector is a noble
warrior fighting against his conscience and better judgment; Aeneas and Antenor are "open traitors unto their
city and also to their king and lord."

The striking characteristics in Chapman's Homer, on
the other hand, are first, that it fixes the interest upon the
Greek camp; and second, that Chapman brutalizes and
roughens the simplicity of the Greek original. In Chapman, Homer's naïveté of speech becomes unredeemed
billingsgate; Homer's temperamental primitives become
arrant cowards, braggarts, and bullies.

Where another writer might have attempted to mediate
between these two irreconcilable accounts, Shakespeare
has seized the essential spirit of each, poetically intensified
it, and hurled both, unmixed and forever unmixable, into
the seething vortex of his play. Thus he produces a milieu
for Troilus and Cressida, the forlorn and fated lovers,
wandering between two worlds: the effete, immoral, over-
refined world of Troy, and the brutal, quarrelsome, cynical world of the Greeks. Paris is on the one side, Diomed
on the other. Shakespeare makes each of these environ-
ments develop its special type figure, emblematic of the
worst in itself. Thersites came to him ready-made out of
Chapman:

The filthiest Greek that came to Troy: he had a goggle eye;
Stark-lame he was of either foot; his shoulders were contract

Into his breast and crookt withal; his head was sharp compact,
And here and there it had a hair. To mighty Thetides
  [Achilles]
And wise Ulysses he retained much anger and disease,
For still he chid them eagerly; and then against the state
Of Agamemnon he would rail. The Greeks in vehement hate
And high disdain conceited him. . . .

Thersites chants an interpretative, accusing chorus to all the Greek scenes. Opposite him, at the other pole of foulness, stands the evil genius of Troy, the Lord Pandarus—Chaucer's Pandarus grown old, impotent, and rotten, but still every inch a lord, sure of welcome in any Merry Monarch's court: urbane, genuinely good-tempered, and still, I insist, likable, with a candy deal of courtesy and a Falstaffian love of young rogues; in fact a Belial than whom "a fairer person lost not heaven." Pandarus and Thersites are the Scylla and Charybdis of the lovers' voyage, and their extremes meet in one only point —in lechery, which they keep shrieking, lisping, and insinuating till the echoes meet and merge like a miasma over the whole play, and all the nobility of life is choked.

Greater scenes and more magnificent lines than some that are found in *Troilus and Cressida* it is agreed that Shakespeare seldom wrote. The question is, what was his purpose? I cannot help imagining that he is, however subconsciously, anatomizing the England of the dying Elizabeth: within the wall, the febrile Essex type of decadent chivalry; without, the strident go-getters of the newer dispensation: Cecil-Ulysses and Ralegh-Diomed. I take it that Shakespeare glimpsed somehow the seriousness of the cleavage between Cavalier and Puritan, sensed in Thersites the lowering shadow of Prynne and the iconoclasts, foresaw in Pandarus the portent of the scandalous Carr, Earl of Somerset. Indeed, when reading the great culminating scene (the second of Act V), in which Troilus, the heartbroken young cavalier, and the shrewd old puritan, Ulysses, are drawn together against a giddy and immoral universe, one may almost feel that the writing is prophetic—that the thing must have happened, not at ancient Troy but forty years after the play was created, on some night when Royalist and Cromwellian met beneath the walls of Oxford.

I do not argue that *Troilus and Cressida* is conscious political allegory, but only that Shakespeare, about 1602, had some vision of the extent to which the Chaucerian delicacy of life was threatened by the two great coarsening influences which in fact were then attacking the nation, and that he conceived upon this theme a very wise, spirited, and subtle play. Before he had quite finished it, I think he realized that it could never hope to carry on the stage. This, it seems to me, and not the presence of an alien hand, accounts for the perfunctoriness of the last scenes of Act V, which like all the rest of the piece are in the poet's genuine style. Had the author been Ben Jonson, he might yet have thrown the work at his audience with the justified boast, "By God, 'tis good, and if you like't, you may." Being, as Jonson called him, the gentle Shakespeare, he appears simply to have withheld it from production and let it pass into the hands of those whom the publishers of 1609 call "the grand possessors"—possibly the same group of his "private friends" who read, and (happy men!) who understood, the Sonnets.

IT is not often that factitious and intrinsic values coincide as they do in the First Folio of Shakespeare's plays. The most generally desired by collectors of all English books, and save for freak rarities the most costly, the Folio is, in fact, doubtless the most important volume ever printed in England. It is the sole source of our knowledge of twenty of Shakespeare's plays: from it we derive the only texts of *Macbeth, Julius Caesar, As You Like It, The Tempest, The Winter's Tale, Twelfth Night, Antony and Cleopatra, Cymbeline,* and twelve other dramas. From it we get also the only authentic texts of two other plays (*Henry V* and *The Merry Wives of Windsor*), and texts distinctly superior to what we should otherwise possess of seven more. Thus, of the thirty-seven plays in the Shakespeare canon, only seventeen would be known at all, and only eight in relatively unimpaired form without the Folio of 1623 and the later editions which owe their existence to it.

On the other hand, only a single play of the thirty-seven —the questionable *Pericles*—is missing from the Folio, and only five can perhaps be said to appear there in texts inferior to those found in the best quartos.

Without the Folio, which was rushed through the press, under conditions of evident difficulty and confusion, about November, 1623, it is, of course, possible that fate might have made amends. The work *might* have been attempted later, with a success that would have dwindled in proportion as the time passed. Shakespearean manuscripts, now provokingly nonexistent, *might* have been permitted to survive. But as the case stands, two thirds of all we know of Shakespeare's writings is known by reason of the exertions of the curious copartnership (to be discussed later) which produced the First Folio.

In a broader, but not more important, aspect the Folio is an epoch-making book. Not merely did it introduce Shakespeare to the world of readers; it also introduced dramatic literature. To an extent scarcely equaled by any other printed volume, it established the claim of modern drama to be regarded as a permanent vehicle of poetry and thought.

In the ordinary Elizabethan view the theater had little connection with polite letters and no claim on the interest of posterity. Dramatic authors were actors' hirelings, and actors were mechanical rogues. A play was sold outright, like a suit of clothes (the staple price being £6), and it was not expected to outwear a season. If printed—and only the smallest number gained such distinction—it was printed with equally ephemeral intention, in unbound quarto form, to sell like a modern popular magazine for sixpence. It was the surprising work of Marlowe, Shakespeare, and Jonson that insensibly raised the prestige of dramatic art and with it the social importance of the actor and the playwright.

The contention that a stage play might be dedicated to a patron, like a work of real literature, was first asserted during the last years of Shakespeare's life. Thus George Chapman, in 1612, ventured to inscribe a quarto edition of his *Widow's Tears* to Mr. John Reed of Mitton in the following words:

"Sir, if any work of this nature be worth the presenting to friends worthy and noble, I presume this will not want much of that value. Other countrymen [that is, foreigners] have thought the like worthy of Dukes' and Princes' acceptations; *Ingiusti Sdegni, Il Pentamento Amoroso, Calisto, Pastor Fido, etc.* (all being but plays) were all dedicated to Princes of Italy. . . . This poor comedy (of many desired to see printed) I thought not utterly unworthy that affectionate design in me; well knowing that your free judgment weighs nothing by the name or form, or any vain estimation of the vulgar; but will accept acceptable matter as well in plays as in many less materials, masking in more serious titles."

So, with a little increased confidence, in 1615, the publisher of the first quarto of Fletcher's *Cupid's Revenge* says: "It is a custom used by some writers in this age to dedicate their plays to worthy persons, as well as their other works; and there is reason for it, because they are the best Minervas of their brain, and express more purity of conceit in the ingenious circle of an act or scene than is to be found in the vast circumference of larger volumes."

The sturdy self-reverence of Ben Jonson, greater even than that of his friend Chapman, first seriously essayed the introduction of acting plays into the library. The 1616 Folio of Jonson's *Works* included nine dramas, craftily reinforced by more conventional literature in the form of epigrams, poems, entertainments, and masques. Gargantuan laughter greeted their appearance. Pray, asked an epigrammatist,

> Pray tell me, Ben, where does the myst'ry lurk?
> What others call a Play, you call a Work.

To which the following left-handed reply was made:

> The author's friend thus for the author says:
> Ben's plays are works, where others' works are plays.

The Folio of Shakespeare followed: the second library edition of English stage plays. Though less arrogant in title, since it avoids the offensive term "Works" and calls itself simply *Mr. William Shakespeares Comedies, Histories, & Tragedies*, it is immensely more venturous in fact. Instead of nine plays, it contains thirty-six, all unsupported by sonnets, poems, or other matter of orthodox kind. Some five hundred copies were printed, of which the strangely large number of 172 still survive the constant handling they have had. The price was set high, at twenty shillings (the Folio has never been cheap), and the justification was complete.

A good-natured jest is reported in a joke book of 1639: "One asked another what Shakespeare's Works were worth, all being bound together. He answered, 'Not a farthing.' 'Not worth a farthing!' said he, 'why so?' He answered that his plays were worth a great deal of money, but he never heard that his works were worth anything at all."

But, "Works" or not, they were read. As early as about 1625, Richard James writes to Sir Henry Bourchier: "A young gentle lady of your acquaintance, having read the works of Shakespeare, made me this question"—an intelligent question concerning the historical Fastolfe and Shakespeare's Falstaff. And Milton wrote in 1630 his famous "Epitaph on the admirable Dramatic Poet, W. Shakespeare," in which he praised "the leaves of thy unvalued [that is, invaluable] book." A reprint of the Folio was required in nine years (1632), whereas Jonson's plays waited a quarter of a century for the second edition.

Two more editions of Shakespeare's plays appeared during the seventeenth century: the Third Folio in 1663–64 and the Fourth in 1685. A very few library editions of other Elizabethan dramatists were produced during this period. Thus Blount, one of the publishers of the first Shakespeare Folio, brought out in 1632 a collection of six of John Lyly's plays under the title, *Six Court Comedies*. In 1633 six of Marston's tragedies and comedies were collected. In 1647 thirty-four previously unprinted plays of the Beaumont-Fletcher canon were issued in folio under the editorship of the dramatist, James Shirley, and in 1679 the second, more complete, Beaumont-Fletcher Folio followed. It is safe to surmise that the favorable acceptance of the Shakespeare Folio was the chief encouragement for all these later ventures.

Otherwise small effort was made for centuries to collect or print in permanent form the dramatic productions of Shakespeare's age. The first collected edition of Massinger appeared in 1761, of Ford in 1811, and of Marlowe in 1826. Peele, Webster, Greene, Shirley, Dekker, Chapman, and Heywood were successively reprinted in the course of the nineteenth century from such contemporary quartos as then survived, and Kyd waited till 1901. That the casual quarto issues in which alone the plays of all these men and many more existed were preserved at all may be ascribed to the fact that the folio editions of Shakespeare, and in less measure of Jonson and Beaumont and Fletcher, gave all the dramatic productions of the age a value they could not otherwise have enjoyed in the eyes of the reading public.

Historically as well as sentimentally, then, the year 1623 has a significance hardly smaller than that of 1564 or 1616. The production of the First Folio was an event of major consequence, whether we regard it as the means whereby the greater part of Shakespeare's work was saved from threatening and not improbable perdition, or whether we view it as the most important thing ever done to further the appreciation of English dramatic literature as a whole. It may be worth while to consider the men who made this history and the conditions that they faced. On both these points recent researches, notably by Mr. Pollard and Mr. Greg, have thrown some interesting light.

The men behind the Folio are a sufficiently various group. Fourteen in all are mentioned in the book itself. Of these, four appear as contributors of eulogistic lines on Shakespeare: first and foremost, of course, Ben Jonson,

whose two copies of verses are familiar, and whose ardor
on behalf of the edition probably arose not only from his
cordial appreciation of the merits of his dead friend, "my
beloved, the author," but also from a natural gladness to
see the overconspicuous novelty of his own "Works" relieved by so unexceptionable a companion volume. Less
notable are the poetical effusions contributed by Hugh
Holland, Leonard Digges, and "I. M." (James Mabbe).
Holland was an aristocratic poet, a well-known member
of the Mermaid Club. The Petrarchan sonnet he contrib-
utes "Upon the Lines and Life of the famous Scenic Poet,
Master William Shakespeare" is hardly worthy of its subject. Holland leans heavily upon alliteration's artful aid:

> . . . done are Shakespeare's days:
> His days are done, that made the dainty plays;

and he closes with a punning conceit which is considerably
better as prophecy than as poetry:

> For though his line of life went soon about,
> The life yet of his lines shall never out.

Digges and Mabbe were both amateurs of Spanish literature and friends of Blount, who made rather a specialty of
Spanish works (including *Don Quixote*), and published
within the year a translation of a novel in that language by
each of them. The odd place their encomiums occupy, between the table of contents and list of principal actors, has
been thought to indicate that they were inserted on short
notice as an afterthought. That of Digges, who later wrote
an expanded version of it for the edition of Shakespeare's
Poems in 1640, was well worth securing. It contains several valuable allusions to the contemporary popularity of
certain of Shakespeare's scenes and an interesting reference to his "Stratford moniment," which, Digges says, the
poet's book will outlast.

One other minor and incidental contributor to the volume must be mentioned, though not *honoris causa*. The title page, it is well known, is doubtfully embellished by a counterfeit presentment of the dead poet—the work of Martin Droeshout. I think that Jonson's lines facing the portrait say quite all that can be said for the effort:

> This Figure that thou here seest put,
> It was for gentle Shakespeare cut.
> . . . Reader, look
> Not on his Picture, but his Book!

Little of the accustomed diffidence was felt about securing patronage for these plays. The editors aimed high and addressed the volume "To the most noble and incomparable pair of brethren, William Earl of Pembroke, *&c.*, Lord Chamberlain to the King's most excellent majesty, and Philip Earl of Montgomery, *&c.*, Gentleman of his Majesty's Bed-Chamber. Both Knights of the most noble Order of the Garter, and our singular good Lords." After speaking of their rashness and the comfort they find in the fact that "your Lordships have been pleased to think these trifles something heretofore, and have prosecuted both them and their author living with so much favor," the writers remark: "There is a great difference whether any book choose his patrons or find them: This hath done both. For, so much were your Lordships' likings of the several parts, when they were acted, as before they were published, the volume asked to be yours." "We," they continue, "have but collected them . . . without ambition either of self-profit or fame: only to keep the memory of so worthy a friend and fellow alive as was our Shakespeare, by humble offer of his plays to your most noble patronage." Since Spenser dedicated *The Fairy Queen* to Elizabeth, a nobler confidence had not been asserted.

It was usual in such cases, the author being dead, that the dedication should be signed by the printer or publisher; but in this case authority and dignity were added by the interposition of two of Shakespeare's chief colleagues in the King's Company, John Heminge and Henry Condell. They sign both the dedication to the earls and the address "To the great variety of Readers"—though there have not been lacking modern critics to conjecture that the actual composition of these admirable bits of prose must have been the work of Ben Jonson, or at least of the bookish publisher Blount.

With a zeal for the material interests of the publishers, rather touching in view of their own avowed freedom from ambition of "self-profit," Heminge and Condell plead for many purchasers, reminding the readers that "the fate of all books depends upon your capacities: and not of your heads alone, but of your purses. Well! it is now public, and you will stand for your privileges, we know: to read and censure. Do so, but buy it first. That doth best commend a book, the stationer says. . . . But, whatever you do, buy. Censure will not drive a trade, or make the jack go."

In a much quoted passage, the sincerity and accuracy of which recent investigations have vindicated, Heminge and Condell go on to say: "It had been a thing, we confess, worthy to have been wished that the author himself had lived to have set forth and overseen his own writings. But since it hath been ordained otherwise, and he by death departed from that right, we pray you, do not envy his friends the office of their care and pain, to have collected and published them; and so to have published them, as where before you were abused with divers stolen and surreptitious copies, maimed and deformed by the frauds and stealths of injurious impostors that exposed them—even those are now offered to your view cured and perfect of their limbs, and all the rest absolute in their numbers as he conceived them."

Mr. Pollard has come effectively to the defense of the sometimes unduly condemned quarto editions, and has shown that they do not by any means all deserve to be set in the rank of the "divers stolen and surreptitious copies" reprobated by the Folio editors. But this necessary recognition of widely variant degrees of grace in the quartos only emphasizes (as Mr. Pollard also shows) the intelligent judgment of Messrs. Heminge and Condell. Of the sixteen plays available in quarto editions, the Folio makes use of only eight, these being the ones which there is inherent reason for believing the most authentic. In five of these cases (*Much Ado, A Midsummer Night's Dream, Richard II, I Henry IV*, and *Titus Andronicus*) the quarto text has been corrected or expanded before being sent to the printer. In the case of eight other plays (*Merry Wives of Windsor, II Henry IV, Henry V, Richard III, Troilus and Cressida, Hamlet, King Lear*, and *Othello*), though quartos were available and obviously convenient, the Folio editors adopted the more conscientious course of ignoring them and printing from manuscript, as they did, of course, with the twenty plays yet unpublished.

The men concerned with the mechanical manufacture of the book are by no means the least interesting group. The title page contains the brief statement: "Printed by Isaac Jaggard and Ed. Blount, 1623." The colophon on the last page is more explicit: "Printed at the Charges of W. Jaggard, Ed. Blount, I. Smithweeke, and W. Aspley." Aspley and Smethwick appear also among the publishers of the Folio of 1632, but their part in the enterprise was relatively small. Aspley, who had once been a partner of Blount's, owned the copyright of *Much Ado* and *II Henry IV*, and may have had some claim on *I Henry IV, Richard*

II, and *Richard III*. Smethwick held the copyright of *Love's Labour's Lost*, *Romeo and Juliet*, and *Hamlet*, with a more dubious claim on *The Taming of the Shrew*. They doubtless received shares in the Folio commensurate with these holdings, but the largest risks and honors in the venture evidently belonged to the two Jaggards, father and son, and to Edward Blount. The younger Jaggard, Isaac, figures as printer, and it was in the Jaggard printing house that the work was done.

Blount, known as the friend of Marlowe and a man of taste, publisher of *Hero and Leander*, Florio's *Montaigne*, and the first English versions of *Don Quixote* and *Guzman d'Alfarache*, was probably the most gentlemanly and literate of the stationers of his time. William Jaggard was one of the most ruffianly, though certainly a shrewd and ardent businessman. It was with Blount, we may cheerfully infer, that Shakespeare's actor colleagues dealt in the matter, and to whom they entrusted the unpublished manuscripts. Blount, accordingly, in conjunction with Isaac Jaggard as his printer (for Blount had no press), registered his copyright, on November 8, 1623, in sixteen Shakespearean plays. The list itemizes accurately and completely all the plays of Shakespeare which had not been previously printed, with the exception of the first and second parts of *Henry VI*, *King John*, and *The Taming of the Shrew*. The explanation of the omitted titles is that "the third part of Henry the Sixt," which is mentioned, pretty certainly means the play that we know as the first part, while the other four plays (second and third *Henry VI*, *John*, and *Shrew*), though not yet printed in their Shakespearean forms, were all represented—in a more or less Pickwickian sense—by quarto prints of the pre-Shakespearean versions. All the sixteen plays registered remained Blount's property and were by him transferred, in 1630, to Robert Allot, the chief publisher of the Second Folio.

William Jaggard had for a long time manifested a felonious interest in Shakespeare's works. In 1599 he caused to be printed a small octavo booklet, entitled *The Passionate Pilgrim. By W. Shakespeare.* This contained two of Shakespeare's sonnets (the first to get into print) and three poems (one a regular and one an irregular sonnet) from *Love's Labour's Lost,* of which a quarto edition had appeared in 1598. Otherwise the little book is made up of poems in which Shakespeare had no discernible interest. In 1612 it reached a third edition, in which Jaggard ventured to swell the volume by calmly annexing two poems out of Thomas Heywood's *Britain's Troy* (printed by Jaggard in 1609), and described the book as "newly corrected and augmented by W. Shakespeare." On this occasion, honest Heywood spoke his mind in words that leave no doubt concerning Jaggard's mechanical and moral imperfections or Shakespeare's opinion on at least the latter point. Heywood's *Apology for Actors* was printed by Nicholas Okes in 1612, and the author appended to it a letter on the subject of Jaggard's enormity of the same year. It runs as follows:

To my approved good friend, Mr. Nicholas Okes.—The infinite faults escaped in my book of *Britain's Troy* by the negligence of the printer, as the misquotations, mistaking of syllables, misplacing half lines, coining of strange and never heard of words, these being without number, when I would have taken a particular account of the *errata*, the printer [Jaggard] answered me, he would not publish his own disworkmanship, but rather let his own fault lie upon the neck of the author. . . . Here, likewise, I must necessarily insert a manifest injury done me in that work, by taking the two epistles of Paris to Helen, and Helen to Paris, and printing them in a less volume ["The Passionate Pilgrim"] under the name of another [Shakespeare], which may put the world in opinion I might steal them from him, and he, to do himself right, hath since published them in his own name. But, as

I must acknowledge my lines not worthy his patronage [Shakespeare's] under whom he [Jaggard] hath published them, so the author [Shakespeare] I know much offended with M. Jaggard that (altogether unknown to him) presumed to make so bold with his name. These and the like dishonesties I know you to be clear of; and I could wish but to be the happy author of so worthy a work as I could willingly commit to your care and workmanship. Yours, ever, THOMAS HEYWOOD.

Jaggard was so far moved, either by Heywood's printed or Shakespeare's vocal objurgations, that he substituted in the unsold copies of *The Passionate Pilgrim* a new title page in which Shakespeare's name is cancelled. If this was a mark of inward grace, it was not permanent. The discoveries of Mr. Pollard and Mr. Greg, less than twenty years ago, have disclosed how Jaggard and a kindred spirit, Thomas Pavier, plotted in 1619 to palm off as Shakespeare's works a group of such putative or derelict dramas as they could lay their hands upon, the book to comprise, probably in the following order: the pre-Shakespearean versions of second and third *Henry VI, Pericles, A Yorkshire Tragedy*, the pirated text of *The Merry Wives of Windsor, The Merchant of Venice, A Midsummer Night's Dream, King Lear*, the bad *Henry V* text, and *Sir John Oldcastle*. Since the two Henry VI plays were combined under the new title of *The Whole Contention between Lancaster and York*, the assortment would have consisted of nine plays, the same number as had appeared three years before in the Jonson Folio. The pirates seem to have been frightened into abstaining from their purpose of publishing this precious collection in a single volume as "Shakespeare's Works," but they brought them out separately, with an apparatus of false dates and fraudulent imprints which fooled the world for near three hundred years.

This was the situation when, four years later, the reputable Blount and the pious actor friends of Shakespeare enlisted Jaggard capital and the Jaggard printing press in the enterprise of the great Folio. Ironically enough, the identical fount of type which perpetrated the forgeries of 1619 was now reset to print the *bona fide* texts. Such a consummation may well have produced unwonted enthusiasm and excitement in the Jaggard establishment. The Folio bears abundant marks of both. It is a grandiose affair, in which money and labor were evidently not grudged, but it was obviously pushed through with much hurry, rattle, and confusion.

As everybody knows, the plays were thrown into three groups with separate pagination: Comedies, Histories, and Tragedies. These divisions are accurate enough, except for *Cymbeline*, which comes at the end of all the tragedies, instead of beside *The Winter's Tale*, as one would expect, in the comedy section. *Troilus and Cressida* and *Timon of Athens* got rudely buffeted, and *Troilus* was nearly omitted altogether. Originally set up to follow *Romeo and Juliet* among the tragedies, it was pulled out again to make place for *Timon*, which fails to fill up sufficient pages and leaves a telltale gap in the numbering; while *Troilus*, with pages unnumbered (save for two accidental survivals from the old pagination) and no place in the table of contents, finally slunk into a no man's land between the last of the history plays and the first of the tragedies.

The chronological incoherence of the order of plays in the comedy and tragedy sections and the erratic manner in which act and scene division is attempted or abandoned are well known. Through all this, as Mr. Pollard subtly argues, one decreasing purpose runs. The editors—Blount, Heminge-Condell, or whoever—"placed unprinted plays in all the important positions [at the opening and close of sections] and hid away those already printed in the middle of them." Thus the comedy section opens with five plays, of which only one, *The Merry Wives of Windsor*, had ever been printed, and that in a pitiably truncated version; and it closes with five other unprinted plays, while in the middle are bunched four plays (*Much Ado, Love's Labour's Lost, Midsummer Night's Dream, Merchant of Venice*) which were available in good quarto editions. Similarly, the ambitious purpose of the editors was to provide act and scene division (not indicated in quartos or manuscripts), and to adapt the stage directions to the needs of the reader rather than the stage prompter; but they lacked time or patience to carry this intention through, doing it best in the plays marked for conspicuous positions. Therefore (to quote Mr. Pollard once more), "The position which a play occupies in the volume offers a very fair index to the amount of care which will be found to have been bestowed upon it."

Proofreading was as spasmodic as might be expected. Printer's errors abound, and divergences between different copies (indicating attempts to purify the text after part of the impression was printed) probably exceed even the Elizabethan average. But these blemishes are venial, the result of honest haste. Most of the misprints are capable of correction, though in their time they made plenty of work for Theobald and his brethren. Whatever their sins of negligence, the printers and editors of the Folio deserve an everlasting praise for resisting the impulse to tamper consciously with Shakespeare's text, even where they must certainly have failed to understand it. On the whole, the text of the book, with all its mechanical blunders, is admirably reassuring and testifies to the truth of what Heminge and Condell say concerning the excellence of the poet's manuscripts: "What he thought he uttered with that easiness, that we have scarce received from him a blot in his papers."

No less haste than that with which the Folio printers worked would have sufficed, in truth, if W. Jaggard were to enjoy the full fruition of his naughty pilferings and depart in the odor of bibliographical sanctity. On November 8, when Blount and Isaac registered their claim—a little unpunctually, it would seem—to the sixteen previously uncopyrighted plays, old Jaggard was blind and near the point of death. His will was proved on the seventeenth of the same month. His last act of which a record remains was to present a Folio, presumably an advance copy, to Augustine Vincent, a crony and ally in one of his printer's wars. The manuscript inscription is extant in a copy lately in possession of Mr. Charles Sibthorp Coningsby: "Ex dono Willi. Jaggard Typographi, a(nn)o 1623."

> Nothing in his life
> Became him like the leaving it. He died
> As one that had been studied in his death
> To throw away the dearest thing he ow'd
> As 't were a careless trifle.

THE SHAKESPEARE TERCENTENARY

A CYNIC with the gift of paradox might expatiate entertainingly on the folly of centenary observations of poets' deaths. Let us thus observe, he might say, the anniversaries of great battles, discoveries, or revolutions—material and specific landmarks of human progress—but why devote particular days or years to the praise of those who truly are not of an age but for all time? and why memorialize that which is least memorable about them—the accident of mortal dissolution?

The Shakespeare celebrations of 1916 have furnished two good answers to such doubts. In the first place, though the poet is for all time, it is not to be expected that he will at all times equally reach the minds of all the people. The rather silly jubilee at Stratford, devised by Garrick in 1769, produced real results in the way of increased appreciation of Shakespeare; and the widespread celebrations of 1916 must likewise have left permanent traces. Not in every year or every decade could such an exhibition of Shakespeareana have been got together as that displayed last summer [1916] in the New York Public Library, or such a stream of visitors drawn to see it. If the tangible result upon the majority of these thousands was no more than what has been modestly claimed for the universal study of Latin and Greek at Eton—a fervent personal conviction of the existence of the matter in question—the exhibition would be well worth all the pains it cost.

And if a very large proportion of the educated public can at any time be awakened to active interest in a poet only by some adventitious reminder, there are also times when even his most devoted followers are likely to grow forgetful. Such was the year 1916. The editors of the splendid Oxford volumes on *Shakespeare's England* explain that the appearance of the book in the middle of the great war was an accident. Anglo-Saxons must have thought it a most happy accident that the claims of the great reconciler and of permanent life values should be so monumentally vindicated in a time otherwise given over to drum and cymbal's din. So, again, for those who can echo Tom Campbell and

> . . . love contemplating—apart
> From all *her* homicidal glory,
> The traits that soften to our heart
> *Germania's* story,

the last *Jahrbuch* of the German Shakespeare Society containing Gerhart Hauptmann's address, "Deutschland und Shakespeare," has offered much needed comfort.

The large amount of valuable published matter inspired by the Shakespeare Tercentenary can be most readily reviewed by distinguishing between those works which are mainly bibliographical in their interest and those of a predominantly literary or historical importance. In the first group belong, of course, the printed catalogues of the excellent Shakespearean exhibitions held in various libraries. England is thus represented by the illustrated catalogues published by the Bodleian and by the John Rylands Library of Manchester, the former a model for beauty of form. For the exhibition of Mr. Marsden J. Perry's collection at Newport, Rhode Island, in June and July, 1916, Mr. George Parker Winship wrote a charming descriptive commentary: *The Redwood Library Guide to an Appreciation of Wm. Shakespeare His Works and Fame.* The particular gems of the Perry collection are one of the two known copies of the earliest edition of the second part of *Henry VI* (*The First Part of the Contention*, etc., 1594) and the famous Edward Gwynn copy of the nine Shakespearean and pseudo-Shakespearean plays issued by Pavier and Jaggard in 1619—the only copy in which these plays are still bound together.

The exhibition at the New York Public Library, April 2–July 15, 1916, was naturally on a larger scale and drew from various sources. Miss Henrietta C. Bartlett prepared an excellent catalogue [1] in which the various items are arranged in five classes: "Shakespeare's Works," "Spurious Plays," "Adaptations of Shakespeare's Plays," "Source Books," and "Allusions to Shakespeare in Contemporary Literature." The bibliographical description of each book is supplemented by anecdotal and critical comment, which makes the work hardly less entertaining than informative. The only defect of which the future user of this catalogue is at all likely to complain is the failure to give any hint regarding the present ownership of the works catalogued. Undoubtedly the silence on this point is intentional, and it is easy to imagine a number of good reasons against discriminating between the different owners. The largest contributors appear to have been the Lenox collection of the New York Public Library, Mr. H. E. Huntington, and Mr. W. A. White. The Library officials, of course, must have full information on record, and it is to be hoped that no student will find serious difficulty in tracing any of the volumes catalogued now that they have been restored to their owners.

In her Introduction Miss Bartlett calls attention to the difference now prevailing in conditions of ownership and accessibility between the rare Shakespeareana in England and in America. In number they are at present very nicely balanced between the two countries; but, whereas in England most of them have at last found permanent resting

1. *Catalogue of the Exhibition of Shakespeareana held at the New York Public Library, April 2 to July 15, 1916, in Commemoration of the Tercentenary of Shakespeare's Death, 1917.*

places in great public libraries, such as the British Museum, the Bodleian, and Trinity College, Cambridge, in the United States a large proportion still belong to private citizens. From the point of view of the humble person who may desire to use such treasures, there are advantages each way. The public institution is undoubtedly the safest conservator and usually the most easily accessible. It is generally better catalogued, and its catalogues have more permanence and broader distribution. On the other hand, the tradition of generosity established by the great English private libraries—now, with the notable exception of the Earl of Ellesmere's, largely dispersed [2]—has been so nobly continued by American owners like Mr. Huntington, Mr. Morgan, and Mr. White, that the serious scholar often finds actually greater opportunity and more helpful assistance as their guest than he can find in the average public institution. There is also, of course, a special charm about the private library, particularly when, like that at Bridgewater House, it has behind it a tradition of centuries; and it might even be questioned whether the great public libraries have done much more for the advancement of scholarship in the department of Elizabethan literature than have the houses of Devonshire and Ellesmere, Huth and Christie-Miller.

Miss Bartlett points out that the rule prohibiting the loan of rare books from one public library to another would make it impossible to assemble in England at present a composite collection equal to that exhibited at New York last summer [1916]. The point might be illustrated by the fact that the arrangers of the John Rylands exhibition were unable to set a single early Shakespearean quarto play by the side of their valuable collection of Folios and their rare editions of the Poems. It is true that the British

2. Since this was written Lord Ellesmere's library at Bridgewater House has been sold to Mr. Huntington and removed to New York.

Museum might have produced from its own unrivaled store an array of Shakespeareana only slightly less complete than that which Miss Bartlett describes, but it would hardly have had the special attractiveness that the New York exhibition gained from the fact that it was a co-operative community affair.

Two very important contributions to Shakespearean bibliography must be regarded as by-products of the American interest in the Tercentenary. In both Miss Bartlett had an honorable part. Her careful work with Mr. White's books disclosed the existence of a hitherto unknown (third) edition of *Richard II* (1598). With characteristic zeal and generosity Mr. White at once produced a reprint of this rare find,[3] to which Mr. A. W. Pollard added an important introduction, arguing that the text of the play was based in the first instance directly upon Shakespeare's manuscript.

The most ambitious of all the bibliographical publications of the year is the *Census of Shakespeare's Plays in Quarto*, 1594–1709, prepared under the auspices of the Elizabethan Club of Yale University by Miss Bartlett and Mr. Pollard.[4] Supplementing the *Census of Folios and Poems* by Sir Sidney Lee, the editors give a detailed list of the known copies (886 in all) of Shakespearean quartos published prior to Rowe's *Shakespeare* of 1709. The work has been done with the utmost care and on the basis of quite unexcelled bibliographical knowledge. It is hardly reckless to doubt whether the list will ever be very materially increased, unless by the discovery of now inaccessible treasures on the continent of Europe. It is interesting to observe that all the copies identified by the editors are now either in British or in American libraries.

Each copy listed in the *Census* is in general elaborately

3. Quaritch, 1916.
4. Yale University Press, 1916.

described as regards condition and ownership, past and present. The only important deficiencies occur in the case of books belonging to the late Lord Ninian Crichton Stuart and to Mr. H. C. Folger. Particular descriptions were unobtainable in the first instance owing to the owner's death in battle, October, 1915. The difficulty of access to Mr. Folger's books is well known to be quite insuperable.[5] However, he has been good enough to furnish the editors with certain details regarding the invisible volumes, which, if not sufficiently complete to accord with the general plan of the book, yet very materially add to what was previously known of his extraordinary collection.

The Introduction to the *Census* is essentially the work of the British collaborator, Mr. Pollard, than whom, it is needless to say, no more competent authority lives. It is a monograph of over thirty close-filled pages, supplementary to the author's well-known work on *Shakespeare Folios and Quartos* (1909), and adding a large amount of most important material. No serious student, however scornful of bibliography—and the number of scorners is healthily waning—can safely overlook Mr. Pollard's discussion of the formation of the various great collections of quartos, the relation between the number of extant copies of early editions and the contemporary popularity of the various plays, and the number of copies originally printed (*ca.* 1,000–1,200). Most important of all is the vindication of the intrinsic textual value of the eighteen "first" quartos (inclusive of the 1599 *Romeo and Juliet* and the 1604 *Hamlet*) as compared with later quartos and even with the Folio. All readers may not be disposed to accept Mr. Pollard's charitable assumption that Heminge and Condell, in sneering at the "stolen and surreptitious copies" which

5. Mr. Folger's books have been available, since his death, to all scholars in the Folger Shakespeare Library in Washington, D.C. [Ed.]

antedated their Folio, had in mind only the two (or possibly five) worst quartos, to which their words might fairly apply; but few will probably refuse to acknowledge that the words are quite unjust in reference to the generality of the quartos. Most persons who have collated early editions of Shakespeare will doubtless agree also with Mr. Pollard's daring conclusion that "The modern editor has nothing to consider save the original readings of the First Quarto and the original readings, right or wrong, introduced by the Folio." This, coupled with our present knowledge—so largely due also to Mr. Pollard—which *were* the first quartos of *The Merchant of Venice*, *A Midsummer Night's Dream*, *King Lear*, and *Henry V*, greatly clarifies the whole textual problem.

The more literary study of Shakespeare has been no less advanced by publications of the tercentenary year. First mention is due to *Shakespeare's England*, in two gorgeous volumes from the Oxford Press. This is followed at a distance by *A Book of Homage to Shakespeare* from the same press. The latter is a "scrapbook," comprising a great number of brief Shakespearean notes by scholars of many lands. *Shakespeare's England* consists of thirty extended essays, all of British authorship, designed to cover the whole range of sixteenth-century English life. Dr. McKerrow's paper on "Booksellers, Printers, and the Stationers' Trade" may be particularly noted as doubtless the best general introduction to the problems of Elizabethan bibliography yet produced. Another of the essays, that on "Handwriting" by Sir E. Maunde Thompson of the British Museum, has already borne further fruit in a separate monograph by the same distinguished authority on *Shakespeare's Handwriting* (Oxford, 1916). The arguments here marshaled to prove that three inserted folios in the manuscript play of *Sir Thomas More* are written in Shakespeare's hand go near to making a certainty of what has hitherto been only an interesting possibility. Additional evidence in the same direction has still more recently been offered by Mr. Percy Simpson in *The Library* (January, 1917).

A useful volume, which, like *Shakespeare's England*, owed to accident its appearance in the tercentenary year, is the translation of a portion of Creizenach's *Geschichte des neueren Dramas, Band IV*, published in London and Philadelphia under the title, *The English Drama in the Age of Shakespeare*. This was almost ready in August, 1914, when the war interrupted its progress. It now appears with a graceful dedication by the English publishers "To the Memory of their Friend and Fellow-Worker, Alfred Schuster, Lieutenant, 4th Hussars (Killed in Flanders, Nov. 20, 1914)." The translation is well done and should be of considerable use, though the omission of Creizenach's long ninth book, containing most of his formal criticism of the plays treated, will make it impossible to employ it as a full substitute for the original.

A number of important American books on Shakespeare appeared in 1916. Two of the most valuable are *Shakespeare's Theater* by Professor A. H. Thorndike of Columbia (Macmillan) and Professor R. M. Alden's variorum edition of the *Sonnets* (Houghton Mifflin). The former gives in some five hundred pages a very compendious summary of what is known concerning theatrical affairs during the reigns of Elizabeth and James, with special reference to two thorny subjects—the history of the various companies of players and the principles of stage presentation. Professor Alden provides students of Shakespeare's Sonnets with what has long been a positive necessity—a complete and reliable compilation of all the important criticism called forth by the most doubt-provoking and bitterly argued of Shakespearean problems.

Two American universities, Columbia and Wisconsin,

published important tercentenary volumes of Shakespearean criticism. The latter is the handsomer in appearance, the former the larger book by a ratio of eighteen to twelve essays. They are further distinguished in that the Columbia contributors have restricted themselves to discussion of aspects of Shakespeare's work, while the Wisconsin critics in some instances go farther afield and treat questions of general Elizabethan interest. Each book offers a distinct addition to knowledge; both naturally contain also matter of an appreciative rather than scientific value. The latter type of article is certainly not less necessary or less suited to the tercentenary occasion. An excellent example is the essay on "The Restoration of Shakspere's Personality" by Professor Brewster, of Columbia. It is quite possible that it would not have occurred to the writer to undertake this acute and judicial review of the constantly changing estimates of the man Shakespeare from the days of the earliest romanticists to the present decade had not his colleagues' desire to commemorate the tercentenary turned his thoughts in that direction. The result is a work of exceptional value to all real students of the poet. Of similar nature are Professor Cunliffe's discussion of the character of Henry V as interpreted by many varying critics, that of Professor Brander Matthews on "Shaksperian Stage Traditions," and, in the Wisconsin volume, the papers on "Some Principles of Shakespeare Staging" (T. H. Dickinson), "Joseph Ritson and Some Eighteenth-Century Editors of Shakespeare" (H. A. Burd), and "Charles Lamb and Shakespeare" (F. W. Roe).

Other American universities have offered such various homage to the occasion that particular mention may appear invidious. If it be permissible for this writer to specify some from which he has profited, he would name Professor Kittredge's Harvard lecture (Harvard University Press); Professor Neilson's paper on "Shakespeare and

Religion," delivered at Yale; the particularly charming jubilee at Brown University, enhanced by a series of lectures by Professor Potter, by an exhibition of Mr. Perry's books, attended with much gracious hospitality to stranger guests, and, finally, by an admirable address of Dr. Woodberry, given in Sayles Hall, April 26, and published by the Woodberry Society; and the unique celebration at the University of Chicago (February 25, 1916), "illustrating the chief types of drama before Shakspere," the handsome program of which contains important material relating to the four pieces performed. The University of North Carolina devoted the April, 1916, issue of its *Studies in Philology* to Shakespearean subjects and has repeated the tribute even more ambitiously in the corresponding number of the 1917 volume. Yale University found inspiration in the Tercentenary for a new teaching edition of the poet (*The Yale Shakespeare*, Yale University Press), of which the completion will require several years.

The pleasing but parlous ambition to render dramatic tribute to the dramatist flourished most beyond academic walls. The best of several playlets of the year is doubtless *Master Will of Stratford* (Macmillan) by Mrs. Louise Ayres Garnett, a Shakespearean night's entertainment, offering an agreeable view of the boy and his mother and a black picture of Sir Thomas Lucy in the year of grace, 1575.

Upon one point the Tercentenary has not brought agreement—the spelling of the poet's name. It is still Shakspere at Chicago and Columbia, Shakespeare at Wisconsin and elsewhere. Many a more important problem, however, has been driven far toward solution; and it will be only the staunchest and mossiest of professors whose Shakespeare lectures of yesteryear will not suffer considerable alteration in 1917.

SHAKESPEARE AND THE
TEXTUS RECEPTUS *

I T is rather paradoxical that Spenser, who "writ no language," as his contemporary Jonson asserted, yet persists for us—when some rather simple allowances are made for odd rime and grammar—as a well of Elizabethan English undefiled; whereas Shakespeare, who wrote racy, colloquial, and sometimes flamboyant Elizabethan, confronts the modern reader in a form which often gives him the aspect of an eighteenth-century classic. The late Dr. McKerrow was not greatly exaggerating when he wrote in an annual Shakespeare lecture of the British Academy: "In spite of the work of the last 150 years, Shakespeare, as he is known in the literature, not only of our own country, but of the world, is still in the main the Shakespeare of Rowe, Pope, Theobald, Johnson, and the other eighteenth-century editors."

McKerrow saw in this the praise of Rowe and his influential successors. Without detracting from the greatness or historic usefulness of their services, I would ask whether it is not time to liberate the poet more completely than has yet been done from the strong web which so remarkably attaches him to the sensibilities, methods, and ideas of a century as remote from his own age as from ours.

The quality about Shakespeare's works which troubled learned readers a century after his death—and troubled them more than his Gothic "bombast"—was the sheer difficulty of understanding him.

Dr. McKerrow has quoted Francis Atterbury's confession to Pope in 1721: "I have found time to read some

* The following essay was read at a meeting of the Modern Language Association in 1945.

parts of Shakespeare, which I was least acquainted with. I protest to you, in a hundred places I cannot construe him: I do not understand him. The hardest part of Chaucer is more intelligible to me than some of those scenes, not merely through the faults of the edition, but the obscurity of the writer, for obscure he is."

Obscure he often is, certainly; and it is a mark of virtue, no doubt, that Pope and his brethren proceeded, with the downright earnestness that distinguished their great age, to make Shakespeare talk sense. But it is discreditable to us, who know so much more of Shakespeare's language and range of ideas, and are fortified on all sides by dictionaries, texts, concordances, grammars, and manuals undreamed of in the past, that we continue to give out as genuine, or at least unimprovable, Shakespeare what is too often only the desperate guess of a graveled eighteenth-century editor.

The sledded Polacks in *Hamlet*, the tired Ingener in *Othello*, the 'lym' or lime-hound who joins the procession of dogs in *Lear* (III, vii, 74) on the invitation of Hanmer, the very, very pea-jock or peacock to which Hamlet compares his uncle, the remarkable ostriches that with their wings baited like eagles having lately bathed (*I Henry IV*. IV, i, 98) seem to be mainly products of the eighteenth-century desire for clear and concrete figure. One could make quite a list of flora and fauna in the plays which the poet would never have recognized, though they still pass almost unquestioned.

As everybody knows, the division of scenes is largely, and their location almost entirely, the work of the early editors. Yet, with hardly a question, we read and teach and reprint the plays as if these things were essentials of Shakespeare's art, though they sometimes distort his dramatic purpose and often totally misrepresent the theater for which he was writing. Only one or two modern editors, and probably not many more teachers, will begin the fourth act of *Hamlet* at any point except the absurd one that a late seventeenth-century actors' Quarto curiously hit upon. No critic or editor known to me appears to doubt that the first scene of Act Third of *I Henry IV* takes place at Bangor, where Hotspur, Worcester, Mortimer, and Glendower, with wives and all their followers, are supposed to be the house guests of the Archdeacon. No Elizabethan could have imagined such a social absurdity, and of course nothing in the text hints at it; but Theobald misunderstood a passage in Holinshed, and no questions were ever asked. In the same play Shakespeare's wonderful pageant of the opening of the Battle of Shrewsbury is destroyed, both for the reader and on the stage, because Pope (and everybody after him) split it at the point of closest cohesion into two scenes. In *Antony and Cleopatra* this kind of thing has proceeded so far that the play is at times nearly as unreadable as it is, on this basis, unactable.

Everybody knows that Pope purified a great deal of Shakespeare's meter, and was abetted by his followers in this dull game. Here—as also in the case of the scenes and speeches which the eighteenth century omitted outright, or degraded to footnotes, because in their view unworthy of a gentleman and a Shakespeare—recent editors have repaired much damage. But it is remarkable how many passages of fine honest prose, like the talk of Hotspur and Kate in *I Henry IV* (II, iii, 74 ff.) or Lear's great speech beginning "Ay, every inch a king" still, in all our editions, hobble along on Popian stilts as alleged verse.

It was, of course, the Folio text that the early editors took as their point of departure. It was all that some of them knew, and it is all we yet have to depend on for half the plays. Yet, where the Folio can be compared with an honest quarto text, one generally finds that it presents a histrionic sophistication of the original. It has myriads of capital letters which an Elizabethan would not have used, and which were an irresistible invitation to the age of Pope to turn plain homespun nouns into baroque allegories and personifications. It has thousands of colons which had the effect of gumming disparate sentences together into something presumably rich and strange, but unintelligible to the common mind. One of the very hardest jobs for the teacher of today is to un-stick these compounds and penetrate to the original meaning after Dr. Johnson has employed his incomparable dialectic upon the amalgam. One hates to do it, of course; for the first effect is disappointment at discovering that the poet is only talking sense and not metaphysic. In this matter of punctuation, candles should be lighted in memory of the late Professor Kittredge, who of all moderns appears to have made the most courageous effort to punctuate the works of Shakespeare according to their plain and pure meaning.

In wording also the Folio often overgilds the Shakespearean lily. It was the Folio that threw that apple of discord among the critics, Othello's "upon this hint I spake"; and the other about the time of scorn's "slow and moving finger"—two fruits, I am sure, not plucked from Shakespeare's garden. It is the Folio that somewhat mouthily expands Othello's simple outburst (as the Quarto has it), "But yet the pity of it, Iago, the pity!" into "But yet the pity of it, Iago! O Iago! The pity of it, Iago!" and heightens his invocation of the mortal engines whose wide throats the immortal Jove's great clamors counterfeit into *rude* throats and *dread* clamors. The Folio causes Iago to come in (V, ii, 317) not "in the *nick*" but "in the *interim*." It kills Oswald in *Lear* with a possibly poetic, but quite unknown, weapon, a "ballow" instead of a plain batoon; and in scores of other places it shows that somebody was improving on the old poet long before the Restoration adapters took up the task.

The process went on like the Pontic sea through the sequence of the Folios and into the eighteenth century, and, curiously, it has felt no retiring ebb in more recent times. The Shakespeare that we still want for our money is the Shakespeare that Johnson edited, that Kemble and Kean and Irving recited, which is, of course, the embellished eighteenth-century Shakespeare. It will be the business of the next generation to accustom our literary palates to the simpler fare that the man of Stratford gave the Elizabethans.

A NEW LIFE OF SHAKESPEARE [1]

THIS important contribution to Shakespearean scholarship should be judged in connection with a couple of sentences in Professor Adams' Preface:

"I have avoided, in so far as possible, prolonged arguments on points that cannot be settled, preferring rather to give my own interpretation of the facts, with the reasons therefor. . . . Although I cannot hope to win unanimous assent to the exact dates I have accepted—some of them are necessarily tentative—I have tried to judge each case in the light of all the available evidence, combined with biographical facts and general laws of probability."

If Professor Adams frequently seems dogmatic beyond what the evidence cited by him justifies, it should be remembered, in the first place, that even 550 pages offer too little space for complete presentation of the arguments respecting the life of Shakespeare and the chronology of his works; and, secondly, that a writer on this subject may easily be led to carry even to excess his desire to avoid the vague and tentative inconclusiveness with which Sir Sidney Lee's popular Life of Shakespeare has been often charged. It will never be said of Professor Adams, as the late Samuel Butler said of Sir Sidney: "My greatest difficulty in dealing with him lies in determining what his opinions really are."

Professor Adams' opinions are stoutly and clearly stated. Most of them will probably carry conviction, or at least compel provisional acceptance, for they are based upon a

1. *A Life of William Shakespeare*, by Joseph Quincy Adams (Houghton Mifflin Co.).

seldom rivaled intensity of application to the study of the literature concerning the Elizabethan drama and stage. No one perhaps has a fuller knowledge both of the original documents and of the fruits of recent investigation, and no one therefore has better right to venture a step in the dark at those many points where the light of establishable fact fails and the searcher is left with the alternative of marking time or trusting to his critical intuitions. We may perhaps have to wait a decade or more before an intelligent opinion is possible concerning the positive accuracy of the author's dicta in a number of these interesting situations.

This is by no means to suggest that the body of the book is not sound. On the contrary, it marks an important advance in knowledge at many points. It exploits much more fully than any earlier life of Shakespeare has been able to do the notable discoveries of the past twenty years in Shakespearean bibliography, and connects them in an often luminous way with the life history of the poet. It makes a distinct contribution to the story of Shakespeare's so-called "lost years" (1585–92) by producing reasons for accepting the usually neglected statement, which Aubrey quoted from Beeston, that the dramatist "had been in his younger years a schoolmaster in the country," and it argues in a highly persuasive manner for a "period of non-dramatic composition" from 1592 till 1594, during which Shakespeare was without theatrical connection and therefore free to devote himself to the production of poems and sonnets. A yet more striking addition to general knowledge is the contention, here rendered very probable, that Shakespeare served his dramatic novitiate, not with the company of Lord Strange, as has been supposed, but with that of Lord Pembroke. The fact that this last conclusion has been independently arrived at by Mr. Crompton Rhodes and by Professor A.

Gaw is a rather remarkable confirmation of its inherent reasonableness.

If one wished to press the complaint that Professor Adams does not always take his readers into his confidence regarding the sources of his information on doubtful points, one might refer to his discussion of the plays in which Falstaff figures. In reference to the substitution of Falstaff's name in the *Henry IV* plays for the original name of "Oldcastle," we are told on page 228: "Shakespeare's gratification at the success of *I* and *II Henry IV*, however, was marred by an unlucky accident. The name he originally gave to Falstaff was Sir John Oldcastle, taken over directly from *The Famous Victories*. There it had provoked no comment. But the extraordinary notoriety of the character as portrayed by Shakespeare led to resentment on the part of Henry Brooke, Lord Cobham, who was a lineal descendant of Sir John Oldcastle, the Lollard martyr. Lord Cobham made complaint, probably to the Master of the Revels, who was responsible for licensed plays; or, possibly, to his near neighbor, the Lord Chamberlain, who had general oversight of dramatic affairs, and who was the patron of the company acting the offending plays. In order to avoid giving further distress to the Cobham family Shakespeare, readily no doubt, agreed to change the name of his comic hero."

A footnote adds that Lord Cobham's resentment was "especially occasioned, it seems, by the performance of the two plays at Court during the Christmas of 1597–98." This seems overprecise, unless Professor Adams has new information concerning the acts and feelings of Lord Cobham. So far as I am aware, the idea of his connection with the change of name is evolved merely from a statement of Rowe (1709), who says: "This part of Falstaff is said to have been written originally under the name of Oldcastle; *some of that family being then remaining*, the Queen was

pleas'd to command him to alter it; upon which he made
use of Falstaff"; and from an earlier manuscript by Dr.
Richard James, who says that "the person with which he
undertook to playe a buffone was not Falstaffe, but Sir
Jhon Oldcastle, and that offence beinge worthily taken
*by Personages descended from his title (as peradventure
by many others allso whoe ought to have him in honourable memorie)*, the poet was putt to make an ignorant
shifte of abusing Sir Jhon Falstophe."

It is possible that Lord Cobham personally intervened
in defense of his ancestor's reputation, though what we
know of that poltroon lord hardly predisposes us to expect such extreme delicacy of sentiment; but if Shakespeare himself felt the particular tenderness which Professor Adams assumes that he felt for the Cobham family
pride, was it not surprisingly thoughtless to proceed in the
soon-following *Merry Wives of Windsor* to make the
jealous Ford assume the name of "Master Brooke" in the
performance of his most asinine parts? *"Enter Foord dis-
guised like Brooke,"* the stage direction reads, and so the
name appears throughout the quarto text; but in the Folio
it had to be altered to "Master Broome," to the ruination
of numerous good puns.

The publication of *I Henry IV* in a good quarto text in
1598 is explained by Professor Adams as a further evidence of Shakespeare's desire to make an *amende honorable* to the Cobham family: "He gave *I Henry IV* to the
press in order to show, in black and white, as it were, that
the fat Knight of Eastcheap was called 'Sir John Falstaff.' " This, however, was not enough. "Thereupon,"
Professor Adams continues, "Lord Cobham, it would
seem, in order to clear the reputation of his ancestor, in-
duced the Admiral's Company to produce a rival two-
part play narrating to the people the 'true life' and martyrdom of the real Sir John Oldcastle." Is this not working

Lord Cobham too hard, since what the Admiral's company did is perfectly explainable on business considerations?

In regard to Shakespeare's authorship of *The Merry Wives of Windsor* Professor Adams remarks: "It is likely that he merely reworked an old manuscript, entitled *The Jealous Comedy*, which had been in the possession of his troupe since 1593." Reasons for the assumed likelihood are not given. The conjecture itself originated with Fleay; recent scholars appear usually to have ignored it or to agree with Greg (*Henslowe's Diary*, ii, 156) that it "rests upon a rather slender basis." After performance before Queen Elizabeth, says Professor Adams, the *Merry Wives* "was also, of course, acted before the public during the winter and spring of 1598." No evidence seems to have been found for so definite, or so early, a date; the play is usually assigned to "*ca.* 1599." "After completing *The Merry Wives* for the Queen," Professor Adams continues, "Shakespeare turned his attention to *Henry V*." The point of the priority of the *Wives* is not further argued, but there seems to be force in the common belief that the use made of Corporal Nym both on the title page and in the text of that play proves that *Henry V* (the only other work in which Nym figures) had already appeared. *Henry V* itself has hitherto been dated with much assurance during the spring or summer of 1599 on account of the evident allusion to Essex' expedition to Ireland as still in progress. Professor Adams states that the play "was placed upon the stage in the earlier half of 1598." In a footnote he explains: "We may easily regard the allusion as a six-line insertion designed to take advantage of the popular excitement attending Essex' departure for Ireland. The history of Falstaff as sketched above makes the date 1598 inevitable." If the history is based upon hypothesis, the inevitability seems hardly clear.

Later Professor Adams informs us (pp. 272, 273) that *Henry V* was produced during the Chamberlain Company's temporary occupancy of the old Curtain Theater, and says, "The inadequacy of its accommodations seems to be glanced at in the Prologue:

> Can this cockpit hold
> The vasty fields of France? or may we cram
> Within this wooden O the very casques
> That did affright the air at Agincourt?

I am unable to find in these lines, or in *Henry V* as a whole, the evidences of true humility. A play so evidently spectacular and ambitious, unique in structure, specially adorned with choruses and strikingly rich in the number and variety of characters and scenes, seems obviously meant for a gala occasion. Professor Adams thinks it written during the most anxious days of Shakespeare's company for presentation in the small, antiquated, and despised Curtain. Acceptance of the Essex allusion at its face value in dating the play (and I know no reason for suspecting it to be a late insertion) gives a meaning to the exuberant and memorial character of the play, for the date of Essex' absence in Ireland (March 27–September 28, 1599) coincides charmingly with the date when Shakespeare's company ended the winter of their discontent and established themselves at the Globe. Professor Adams quotes the document of May 16, 1599, which records the new playhouse: "*una domo de novo edificata . . . in occupacione Willielmi Shakespeare et aliorum.*" "Unquestionably," as Mr. Adams remarks (p. 287), "before the end of the summer of 1599 the Lord Chamberlain's Men had moved from the Curtain to their new home, 'the glory of the Bank.'"

The proofreading for the volume has been carefully done, though it happens that page 1 contains a misprint: "was a most [*i.e.,* almost] a commonplace," and page 4 another: "yielded no other illusion [*i.e.*, allusion] to this William Sakeespee."

It would be too much to expect that so plain-spoken and venturous a book upon a subject so important and so disputed should please all readers at all points. But it is certain that the volume will add largely to the already more than enviable position which Professor Adams has made for himself as an expositor of the Shakespearean age. The last paragraph of the author's Preface will doubtless add still further to the envy which Professor Adams' friends cannot but feel when they contemplate his fortunate and merited position:

"Finally, to Mr. August Heckscher, of New York City, I wish to record a special obligation. Through his bounty in establishing at Cornell University the Heckscher Foundation for the Advancement of Research I came to be relieved for a time from the routine of classroom instruction in order that I might complete my investigations and prepare my manuscript for the press. But for this welcome relief I should have had to defer publication for some years."

SOLILOQUY IN A SHAKESPEAREAN CLOISTER [1]

THERE is something suggestive of the longer poems of Browning in the repetitious but impressive volumes in which Professor Dover Wilson narrates his intellectual adventures with the text of *Hamlet*. He tells us everything: his ardors in pursuit, his faith in a science not untinged with clairvoyancy; even, in much detail, his false starts and retractions. He is a very clever, candid, learned scholar and a most engaging talker. His industry and obstinacy are as immense as if he were some humanist of the Renaissance, and his contempt for common opinion belongs to that era. The contribution he brings is by no means small. Students will long be in his debt for his minute cataloguing of all the bibliographical data and his wholehearted championship of the *Hamlet* second Quarto against the first Folio. This needed badly to be done, and he has done it with ardent, if provocative, ingenuity.

Those who read the first volume of his *Manuscript*, in which he tacks up his theses concerning the relation of the bad Quarto of 1603, the good one of 1604–5, and the Folio of 1623 to one another and to what Shakespeare wrote, will have the pleasant feeling of assisting at an important ceremony. Mr. Dover Wilson explains, justly enough, that the text which the benighted nineteenth century left us is unscientific, and he promises one vastly more definitive. He then tells a dramatic story, based upon his reading of bibliographic clues. The Folio *Hamlet*, upon which pre-

1. *The Manuscript of Shakespeare's Hamlet and the Problems of Its Transmission*, by J. Dover Wilson, 2 vols. (Macmillan Co.). *Hamlet*, ed. by John Dover Wilson (Macmillan Co.).

vious editors have mainly relied, is one of the faultiest of
Shakespeare's works, printed (he thinks) from a careless
copy made about 1622 from the Globe Theater prompt-
book, which in its turn was an abridged and altered copy
of Shakespeare's manuscript. This original manuscript,
however, was itself put into the hands of the compositor
who set up the 1604–5 Quarto, while the 1603 Quarto
represents a pirated reconstruction from memory of the
promptbook. It should follow, then, that the second
Quarto gives us the play in its most authentic form, nothing intervening between it and Shakespeare except the
compositor's mistakes and later misguided revisions by the
printer's proofreader. However, the compositor was a
very poor workman, and he made a mess of Shakespeare's
difficult handwriting. Therefore, as Mr. Dover Wilson is
honestly careful to emphasize, recourse must be had continually to the less immediate Folio, and where possible to
the truncated text of 1603, to explain the blunders of Q2
—the second Quarto.

This is admirably lucid, but it is not equally certain at
all points. Mr. Dover Wilson is to be credited with a
courageously simple series of working hypotheses, neatly
presented and skilfully fitted together; but the hypotheses
are not all provable, and they are not invariably the most
reasonable ones for explaining the various data. We must
expect to hear many other interpretations of the clues
which Mr. Dover Wilson has collected, and to see more
ink flow, before much actual reality attaches to the figures
he describes: "Scribe C," for example, producing for Jaggard's printers a transcript "so bad that it cannot possibly
have served as prompt-book in any reputable theatre," "a
slap-dash person," who "often allowed his pen to run
straight on without checking what he wrote with that
from which he was copying," or the compositor of Q2, a
hurried, gasping fellow, "a learner or a young journeyman,

a compositor who *cannot* work quickly because he has not mastered his craft," and probably a Welshman to boot; a "fool, simple to transparency," of whom Mr. Dover Wilson happily thinks, "we may almost steal his eyes and watch Shakespeare's pen moving across the paper."

If there is much that is rather fanciful about this reconstruction of the crime perpetrated upon Shakespeare's *Hamlet*, there is certainly much that is both new and sound. The sad thing is that after so justly upbraiding earlier editors for failing to go to the bottom of the textual philosophy, and after delving so deeply into it himself, Mr. Dover Wilson has in the end to do much as they did, and as every other editor of *Hamlet* must. He, too, must piece together his text from the first Folio and Q2, and when in dire distress must consent to receive aid even from the untouchable Q1. For say what one so rightly may of the dubious pedigree of the Folio copy, it often gives the unquestionably better reading. And laud the legitimate Q2 as you will, it nevertheless prints stuff that would make Mr. Shaw's Eskimo demand his money back if delivered to him as Shakespeare's work. Mr. Dover Wilson recognizes this, of course, and he puts the truth in a noble sentence: "The final arbiter in any particular textual decision must be the judgment and taste of the editor who makes it."

By this principle his text of *Hamlet* will, I fear, be generally condemned; not perhaps for essential lack of "judgment and taste," but for the preconception in favor of Q2 which often suspends them and makes the worse appear the better reason. Of course, the reviewer must be more condemned who delivers such listless cheers for this impressive work without substantiating his unfaith. But to do justice to the text Mr. Dover Wilson offers us would require discussion of the remarkably large number of readings in which it differs from the conventional one and would take a book not much shorter than one of his. One would be continually applauding his resourcefulness and less frequently adopting his conclusions. I can only indicate the courage of his convictions by showing what he makes of a few well-known lines:

> O, that this too too *sullied* flesh would melt.

Both Quartos have "sallied," the Folio "solid."

> Fall a-cursing like a very drab: A *stallion!*

So in Q2; "scullion" in the Folio.

> The terms of our estate may not endure
> Hazard so near 's as does hourly grow
> Out of his *brawls.*

This also is Q2, except the last word, which is Mr. Dover Wilson's emendation for "browes" in that text. "Braves" would perhaps be better; but many will continue to prefer the Folio's "lunacies" to either.

> Why this is *bait* and salary, not revenge.

The italicized word is again the editor's effort to make Q2 talk sense; that text reads "base and silly," the Folio "hyre and Sallery."

> This realm dismantled was
> Of Jove himself, and now reigns here
> A very, very—*peacock.*

Both texts have "paiock," probably Spenser's word, "patchock," likelier surely than "peacock" for Hamlet's "king of shreds and patches."

> O *God*, Horatio, what a wounded name!

"How true, Watson!" as another detective used to say.

A very famous passage in the first scene of the play offers a good example of Mr. Dover Wilson's textual ingenuity.

It happens to be found only in Q2, and so involves no conflict of readings. Hitherto the passage has always been printed thus:

> In the most high and palmy state of Rome,
> A little ere the mightiest Julius fell,
> The graves stood tenantless and the sheeted dead
> Did squeak and gibber in the Roman streets:
> As stars with trains of fire and dews of blood,
> Disasters in the sun; and the moist star
> Upon whose influence Neptune's empire stands
> Was sick almost to doomsday with eclipse:
> And even the like precurse of fierce events,
> As harbingers preceding still the fates
> And prologue to the omen coming on,
> Have heaven and earth together demonstrated
> Unto our climatures and countrymen.
> *Enter Ghost again.*

The fifth line follows awkwardly after the fourth, and previous editors have commonly assumed that the printer of the second Quarto skipped a line here—something which Mr. Dover Wilson proves him all too easily capable of, citing twenty-nine instances of omitted lines and half lines in this Quarto. But Mr. Dover Wilson prefers another explanation here. He lifts the last five verses and neatly inserts them between line four and line five. "What can be wrong with the following?" he asks triumphantly. And indeed it looks very brilliant, as anyone can see for himself by reading the passage in the sequence indicated.

But two things are fatally wrong with it. First, it mercilessly dislocates the "stars with trains of fire and dews of blood" from the other omens of Caesar's death to which they belong. Compare North's translation of the passage in Plutarch's Life of Caesar—"fires in the element and spirits running up and down in the night"—and the parallels in *Julius Caesar:*

> . . . Never till now
> Did I go through a tempest dropping fire,

and

> Fierce fiery warriors fought upon the clouds
> In ranks and squadrons and right form of war,
> Which drizzled blood upon the Capitol.

What is more important, it assumes that Shakespeare passed over his obvious cue for the Ghost's entrance in the majestic words about the "prologue to the omen coming on, . . . Unto our climatures and countrymen"—which so perfectly echo the close of one of the great omen speeches in *Julius Caesar*,

> For I believe they are portentous things
> Unto the climate that they point upon,—

in order to give climactic emphasis to the description of a lunar eclipse. That is, Mr. Dover Wilson banishes an anacoluthon—a common Elizabethan beast, not very harmful to poetry, and besides (if one happens not to like it) easily riddable through lighter bibliographic exorcism— by invoking a rip-roaring anticlimax that tears the whole passage into bloody gobbets.

It is a sorry thing to write thus grudgingly on a work which every student of *Hamlet* is going to use with profit, for it is indeed beset with brilliances; but its bibliographical deductions are constantly leaning out beyond the power of their supports, and its text (human nature being what it is) is going to remind some readers of what Bentley said to Pope and what Bentley did to Milton.

SIR WALTER RALEGH AS POET
AND PHILOSOPHER *

WHEN Sir Walter Ralegh was beheaded, October 29, 1618, there died the last of the Elizabethan romanticists. He outlived his age, and came in the end to suffer by the defects of the very virtues which had made him great.

He has a vast deal in common with each of his romantic colleagues, Sidney, Spenser, and Marlowe. He shares Sidney's courtly brilliance and chivalry, Spenser's political imagination, and Marlowe's luminous independence of mind. He is more like each of the three than any of them was like another. He had been acquainted with them all: with Sidney at the intriguing court, with Spenser in Irish solitudes, with Marlowe at the Mermaid, or wherever else in London speculative and daring thought ran freest. Of the four, Ralegh is the least perfect in his literary work and in his life. In the elements of greatness he was hardly inferior to the greatest of them, but these elements did not so mix in him as to make him the consummate man and artist that Sidney, that Spenser, and even Marlowe each had been.

For this very reason there is a profit in studying Ralegh's mind. The forces of Elizabethan romanticism are seen in him not fused, but in divergence, not in harmony, but in conflict. Ralegh's imagination destroyed nearly as much as it created. It is easier in his case than in Sidney's, Spenser's, or Marlowe's to analyze, and—if one has the heart for it—to dissect.

He began his poetic career with entire appropriateness. While sojourning at the Middle Temple he wrote a com-

* Lecture before the Tudor and Stuart Club, February 24, 1938.

mendatory poem [1] on *The Steel Glass* of George Gascoigne, the soldier poet who had his portrait painted bowing the knee before Queen Elizabeth, with a quill pen in his ear, a lance in one hand, and a book in the other, and who adopted as his motto: *Tam Marti quam Mercurio.* No one in England might more properly have succeeded to Gascoigne's motto than Ralegh. Mars and Mercury were ever contending for his allegiance.

RALEGH's poetry is less romantic than his prose. The one had its chief inspiration in the emulation and repinings of his life at court; the other on the battlefield or voyage of discovery, or in his prison cell. There is in the poetry more of his mind, which was fierce, swift and restless as a bird of prey; in his prose there is more of his grave and steadfast heart.

His poems are intensely interesting and characteristic—though not characteristic of the whole man. They are unsurpassed in their own peculiar way, but the best of them have little in common with the work of Ralegh's great romantic brethren. They are highly poignant, often bitter or defiant, savoring more of fierce insight than of ordered meditation. They are rich in epigram and very clever in conceit, and they have a tang that makes them unforgettable. They reveal, as Sir Edmund Chambers has said,[2] a "fundamental brainwork, a power of concentrated phrasing, which was only too rare among his contemporaries"—except, one might add, that junior contemporary, John Donne, whose intuitive lyric strangenesses (but *not* his "not keeping of accent") Ralegh seems often to be

1. Printed in A. M. C. Latham, *The Poems of Sir Walter Ralegh* (1929), p. 27. The text of Ralegh's poems is peculiarly uncertain. The passages quoted in this essay generally, but not invariably, follow Miss Latham's readings.

2. "The Disenchantment of the Elizabethans," in *Sir Thomas Wyatt and Some Collected Studies,* 1933.

preluding. "The Lie" is a bewildering series of rapier thrusts:

> Say to the court, it glows
>   And shines like rotten wood;
> Say to the church, it shows
>   What's good, and doth no good:
> If church and court reply,
> Then give them both the lie.
>
>   .   .   .   .   .
>
> Tell men of high condition,
>   That manage the estate,
> Their purpose is ambition,
>   Their practice only hate.
> And if they once reply,
> Then give them all the lie.
>
>   .   .   .   .   .
>
> Tell fortune of her blindness;
>   Tell nature of decay;
> Tell friendship of unkindness;
>   Tell justice of delay:
> And if they will reply,
> Then give them all the lie.[3]

The epitaph on Leicester is cool assassination of the dead man's memory:

Here lies the noble warrior that never blunted sword;
Here lies the noble courtier that never kept his word;
Here lies his excellency that governed all the state;
Here lies the Lord of Leicester that all the world did hate.[4]

Equally biting, but in nobler key, is the famous passage said (however fancifully) to have been written the night before his death and found in his Bible:

3. Latham, *op. cit.*, pp. 45–47.
4. *Ibid.*, p. 114.

Even such is time, that takes in trust
  Our youth, our joys, and all we have,
And pays us but with age and dust;
  Who, in the dark and silent grave,
When we have wandered all our ways,
Shuts up the story of our days;
But from this earth, this grave, this dust,
My God shall raise me up, I trust! [5]

Very applicable to Ralegh's poems are the words of Shelley:

Our sincerest laughter
With some pain is fraught:
Our sweetest songs are those that tell of saddest thought.

Like Othello, he did "agnize a natural and prompt alacrity" he found in hardness. He is often gayest (if the word can ever be used of him) when contemplating the mortal dissolution which so constantly overhung him. There is an unforgettable combination of defiance and mystic fervor in his romantic poem, "Sir Walter Ralegh's Pilgrimage":

Give me my scallop-shell of quiet,
  My staff of faith to walk upon,
My scrip of joy, immortal diet,
  My bottle of salvation,
My gown of glory, hope's true gage;
And thus I'll take my pilgrimage.
        .   .   .   .   .
Blood must be my body's balmer;
  No other balm will there be given
Whilst my soul, like a white palmer,
  Travels to the land of heaven;
Over the silver mountains,
Where spring the nectar fountains:
  And there I'll kiss

5. *Ibid.*, p. 64.

The bowl of bliss;
And drink mine everlasting fill
Upon every milken hill.
My soul will be a-dry before;
But after, it will ne'er thirst more.

.   .   .   .   .

Then by the happy blissful way
   More peaceful pilgrims I shall see,
That have shook off their gowns of clay,
   And go apparelled fresh like me.
      I'll bring them first
      To slake their thirst
And taste of nectar suckets,
      At those clear wells
      Where sweetness dwells,
Drawn up by saints in crystal buckets.[6]

Even in his love songs there is a note of scornful dubiety;
and his address to his beloved son does not mask the grin-
ning death's head that Ralegh saw behind all the masques
and mummeries of the world:

Three things there be that prosper all apace,
   And flourish while they grow asunder far;
But on a day, they meet all in one place,
   And when they meet, they one another mar.
And they be these; the Wood, the Weed, the Wag:
The Wood is that which makes the gallows tree;
The Weed is that which strings the hangman's bag;
The Wag, my pretty knave, betokens thee.
Now mark, dear boy—while these assemble not,
Green springs the tree, hemp grows, the wag is wild;
But when they meet, it makes the timber rot,
It frets the halter, and it chokes the child.[7]

Three of Ralegh's happiest poems were inspired by his
three friends, Sidney, Spenser, and Marlowe. The reply

6. *Ibid.*, p. 43.
7. *Ibid.*, p. 102.

to Marlowe's song of the Passionate Shepherd, which achieved a popularity almost equal to that of the original, comes as near to lightheartedness as anything that Sir Walter wrote. It declares, indeed, the impracticality of Marlowe's pure romance, but pays a real and wistful tribute to its loveliness:

> If all the world and love were young,
> And truth in every shepherd's tongue,
> These pretty pleasures might me move
> To live with thee and be thy love.
> But time drives flocks from field to fold,
> When rivers rage and rocks grow cold; . . .
> The flowers do fade, and wanton fields
> To wayward winter reckoning yields . . .
>
> .   .   .   .   .
>
> But could youth last, and love still breed;
> Had joys no date, nor age no need;
> Then those delights my mind might move
> To live with thee and be thy love.[8]

Ralegh's epitaph on Sidney is worthily characteristic of the author. It lacks the emotional warmth of Spenser's praise of Sidney, but it speaks of him nobly, as only one high and soldierly spirit could speak of another. "A king gave thee thy name," says Ralegh; "a kingly mind,—That God thee gave." "Kent thy birthdays, and Oxford held thy youth. . . ."

> Whence to sharp wars sweet honour did thee call,
> Thy country's love, religion, and thy friends;
> Of worthy men the marks, the lives, and ends,
> And her defence, for whom we labour all.
>
> .   .   .   .   .
>
> What hath he lost that such great grace hath won?
> Young years for endless years, and hope unsure

8. *Ibid.*, p. 40.

> Of fortune's gifts for wealth that still shall dure:
> O happy race, with so great praises run! [9]

Ralegh's sonnet in praise of Spenser's great poem, which he calls "A Vision upon this Conceit of The Fairy Queen," is (out of hundreds) the most adequate contemporary tribute to that work, and is itself one of the great sonnets of the language:

> Methought I saw the grave where Laura lay,
> Within that temple where the vestal flame
> Was wont to burn: and, passing by that way,
> To see that buried dust of living fame,
> Whose tomb fair Love and fairer Virtue kept,
> All suddenly I saw the Fairy Queen,
> At whose approach the soul of Petrarch wept;
> And from thenceforth those graces were not seen,
> For they this Queen attended; in whose stead
> Oblivion laid him down on Laura's hearse. . . .[10]

Evidently (as others have pointed out) Milton was indebted to this sonnet when he wrote the great one which begins, "Methought I saw my late-espoused saint." And it gives one a high pleasure to know, from the other, more personal, sonnet that Ralegh appended to the one from which I have just quoted, that this poet—sometimes so like Donne in voice and thought—appreciated the incomparableness of *The Fairy Queen*. "Of me," says Ralegh to Spenser,

> no lines are lov'd, nor letters are of price,
> Of all which speak our English tongue, but those of thy
> device.[11]

This is a requital, not altogether insufficient, for the many testimonials which Spenser has left of his gratitude

9. *Ibid.*, pp. 32–34.
10. *Ibid.*, p. 30.
11. *Ibid.*, p. 31.

for Ralegh's friendship and his admiration of his genius; for Spenser's dedicatory sonnet to Ralegh, and his inscribing of the important explanatory letter, "expounding his whole intention in the course of" *The Fairy Queen* "to the Right noble, and valorous, Sir Walter Raleigh knight"; for the winning picture of the Shepherd of the Ocean in "Colin Clout's Come Home Again" and the allegorical warning of Clarion in "Muiopotmos"; for the stirring and pathetic scenes in which the squire Timias mirrors the loyal chivalry of Sir Walter, and finally for the modest and appreciative stanzas, prefatory to the third book of *The Fairy Queen*, in which Spenser praises Ralegh's poetical tribute to Queen Elizabeth at the expense of his own:

> How then shall I, Apprentice of the skill,
> That whylome in diuinest wits did raine,
> Presume so high to stretch mine humble quill?
>
> .   .   .   .   .
>
> But if in liuing colours, and right hew,
> Your selfe you couet to see pictured,
> Who can it doe more liuely, or more trew,
> Then that sweet verse, with Nectar sprinkeled,
> In which a gracious seruant pictured
> His *Cynthia*, his heauens fairest light?
> That with his melting sweetnesse rauished,
> And with the wonder of her beames bright,
> My senses lulled are in slomber of delight
> But let that same delitious Poet lend
> A little leaue vnto a rustick Muse. . . .

Ralegh's *Cynthia*, his one long poem, we do not really possess. It was never printed, and, as Sir Edmund Chambers reminds us, "was already lost by the middle of the seventeenth century." We can only conjecture, as Sir Edmund does: "You can guess at the theme, with its fine central image of the mistress swaying the hopes and fears of the lover, as the moon sways the ebb and flow of the tides. The lover is both shepherd and mariner; the moon now rides remote and inaccessible among the cloud drifts; now descends to hang like a golden lamp upon the tree-tops as in that serene Latmian night, when Diana came down to sleep with Endymion. We do not know what Ralegh made of it; we should gladly know. Spenser tells us that it was the music of 'the summer's nightingale.' " [12]

All that we do possess is an addendum of 550 lines, which somehow fell into Cecil's fingers and came to light when Hatfield House was gone over. It is not likely that this fragment, composed in profound despair, represents favorably the merits of the earlier work. It is a cloudy and somber performance, but touched with grandeur and deep feeling. The poet now writes "the thoughts of passed times," which

> like flames of hell
> Kindled afresh within my memory
> The many dear achievements that befell
> In those prime years and infancy of love
> Which to describe were but to die in writing.[13]

He recalls the thrilling uncertainties of his service of Elizabeth in the days when he set out

> To seek new worlds for gold, for praise, for glory,
>   To try desire, to try love sever'd far.
> When I was gone, she sent her memory,
>   More strong than were ten thousand ships of war.[14]

In words that remember Spenser he describes the queen's anger:

> A queen she was to me, no more Belphebe;
>   A lion then, no more a milkwhite dove;

12. Chambers, *op. cit.*, p. 196.
13. Lines 166–170 (Latham, *op. cit.*, pp. 82, 83).
14. Lines 61–64.

A prisoner in her breast I could not be,
She did untie the gentle chains of love.

· · · ·

It's now an idle labour and a tale
    Told out of time, that dulls the hearer's ears,
A merchandise whereof there is no sale.[15]

Mordantly he pictures his present forlorn state:

But as a body violently slain
    Retaineth warmth although the spirit be gone,
And by a power in nature moves again,
    Till it be laid below the fatal stone.

· · · ·

So my forsaken heart, my wither'd mind,
    Widow of all the joys it once posses'd,
My hopes clean out of sight, with forced wind
    To kingdoms strange, to lands far off, address'd,
Alone, forsaken, friendless on the shore,
    With many wounds, with death's cold pangs embrac'd,
Writes in the dust, as one that could no more,
    Whom love, and time, and fortune, had defac'd.[16]

In the following stanzas he seems even to prophesy the
History of the World and the circumstances in which it
was written:

As if, when after Phoebus is descended,
    And leaves a light much like the past day's dawning,
And, every toil and labour wholly ended,
    Each living creature draweth to his resting,
We should begin by such a parting light
    To write the story of all ages past,
And end the same before th' approaching night.[17]

Defiant, volatile, darkly imaginative and jauntily reckless, Ralegh as he is manifested in these poems was indeed

15. Lines 327–330, 357–359.
16. Lines 73–76, 85–92.
17. Lines 97–103.

a man after Queen Elizabeth's heart. The reasons for the immense fascination he exerted and the deadly enmities he provoked are equally apparent. His poems as a whole are radically different from any others in English literature: they can hardly be forgotten by anyone who reads them. In a sense they are superficial; they usually show the surface and not the depths of his personality, but their superficiality is impressive and oddly sinister. It is the froth that rises where unplumbed waters break on adamant.

THE breadth and depth of Ralegh's genius are best revealed in his prose, into which he put more of his heart and soul than went into his brilliant verse—and which alone he intended for the English nation and for posterity. The difference is worth repeating; it is the difference between the bagpipe and the organ. Ralegh was a daring and accomplished master of both. The one is dashing, shrill, and provocative; the other of a sonorous dignity which few English writers have equaled. One famous sentence of Ralegh's stands in all good anthologies as the *ne plus ultra* of prose eloquence, matchable with the best of Sir Thomas Browne or De Quincey:

O eloquent, just, and mighty Death! whom none could advise, thou hast persuaded; what none hath dared, thou hast done; and whom all the world hath flattered, thou only hast cast out of the world and despised: thou hast drawn together all the far-stretched greatness, all the pride, cruelty, and ambition of man, and covered it all over with these two narrow words, *Hic jacet!* [18]

This is the rich and solemn melody to which is set nearly all of Ralegh's formal prose. In his letters we find often the more superficial fierceness habitual to the poems. Here,

18. *History of the World* (1614), p. 669. This sentence, the last but one in the book, should be read in connection with the paragraph that precedes it.

for example, is Elizabeth's discredited wooer, writing from prison in 1592 to Sir Robert Cecil:

My heart was never broken till this day, that I heard the Queen goes away so far off,—whom I have followed so many years with so great love and desire, in so many journeys, and am now left behind her, in a dark prison all alone. . . . I that was wont to behold her riding like Alexander, hunting like Diana, walking like Venus, the gentle wind blowing her fair hair about her pure cheeks, like a nymph; sometime sitting in the shade like a Goddess; sometime singing like an angel; sometime playing like Orpheus. Behold the sorrow of this world! Once amiss hath bereaved me of all.[19]

And here is the practiced and deadly courtier, giving the *coup de grâce* to his fallen rival, Essex (again to Cecil, in 1600):

Sir,—I am not wise enough to give you advice, but if you take it for a good counsel to relent towards this tyrant, you will repent it when it shall be too late. His malice is fixed and will not evaporate by any your mild courses. For he will ascribe the alteration to her Majesty's pusillanimity and not to your good nature. . . . Lose not your advantage; if you do I read your destiny.[20]

This is Ralegh the opportunist and the realist. It is Ralegh as his enemies saw him at court, the man of whom Coke could venture to say "Thou hast a Spanish heart, and thyself art a spider of Hell."

What the gypsy palmists say of the lines of the two hands might be said of the two sides of Ralegh's work. One shows the spirit with which he was born, and which never ceased to be fundamental in him—a high romantic spirit. The other shows what he made himself when under the influence of courtly feud and self-seeking. The lower

19. *Ralegh's Letters,* ed. E. Edwards (1868), p. 51.
20. *Ibid.,* p. 222.

voice sounds often in what he wrote on impulse without view to publication. We hear the higher voice when he looks beyond the court and writes consciously for posterity. Prose is then his language, and he speaks a noble tongue. His greatest prose writings—the *History of the World*, the *Discovery of Guiana*, and the *Last Fight of the Revenge*—are splendid monuments of his romantic spirit. They show him to have been a deeply original thinker and moralist, a glorious patriot, and an enthusiastic amateur of the marvels of life.

As a moral philosopher Ralegh is highly impressive. Witness his dignified and subtle reasoning against the contemporary code of the duello—the practice of dueling over the giving of the lie:

But now for "the lie" itself, as it made the subject of all our deadly quarrels in effect; to it I say that whosoever giveth another man the lie, when it is manifest that he hath lied, doth him no wrong at all; neither ought it to be more heinously taken than to tell him he hath broken any promise which he hath otherwise made. . . . On the other side, he that gives any man the lie, when he himself knows that he, to whom it is given, hath not lied, doth therein give the lie directly to himself. And what cause have I, if I say that the sun shines when it doth shine, and that another fellow tells me I lie for it's midnight, to prosecute such an one to death for making himself a foolish ruffian and a liar in his own knowledge? [21]

The Preface to the *History of the World* contains a praise of history worthy of comparison with Sidney's praise of poetry:

True it is, that among many other benefits, for which it hath been honored; in this one it triumpheth over all humane knowledge, That it hath given us life in our understanding, since the world itself had life and beginning, even to this day;

21. *History of the World*, p. 468 (Bk. V, Ch. 3, Sec. 17.2).

yea, it hath triumphed over time, which besides it nothing but eternity hath triumphed over: for it hath carried our knowledge over the vast and devouring space of many thousands of years, and given so far and piercing eyes to our mind that we plainly behold living now, as if we had lived then, that great World, *Magni Dei sapiens opus,* the wise work (saith Hermes) of a great God, as it was then, when but new to itself.[22]

With an august eloquence rarely more impressively employed Ralegh points the great moral which he derives from the course of human history: the folly of ruthless ambition, the fallacy of the principle that might makes right.

For who hath not observed [he asks] what labor, practice, peril, bloodshed, and cruelty the Kings and Princes of the world have undergone, exercised, taken on them, and committed, to make themselves and their issues masters of the world? And yet hath Babylon, Persia, Egypt, Syria, Macedon, Carthage, Rome, and the rest no fruit, flower, grass, nor leaf springing upon the face of the earth of those seeds. No, their very roots and ruines do hardly remain.[23]

In a brilliant survey of English history, he shows how the wages of sin has been death in the cases of Henry I, Edward II, Richard II, Henry IV, Henry VI, Richard III, and finally Henry VIII:

Now for King Henry the Eight. If all the pictures and patterns of a merciless prince were lost in the world, they might all again be painted to the life out of the story of this king. For how many servants did he advance in haste (but for what virtue no man could suspect), and with the change of his fancy ruined again, no man knowing for what offence? To how many others of more desert gave he abundant flowers from whence to gather honey, and in the end of harvest burnt

22. *Ibid.,* Preface, sig. A2.
23. *Ibid.,* sig. A2 verso.

them in the hive? How many wives did he cut off and cast off, as his fancy and affection changed? How many princes of the blood . . . with a world of others of all degrees . . . did he execute! . . . What laws and wills did he devise, to establish this kingdom in his own issues! using his sharpest weapons to cut off and cut down those branches which sprang from the same root that himself did. And in the end (notwithstanding these his so many irreligious provisions) it pleased God to take away all his own, without increase; though for themselves in their several kinds all princes of eminent virtue.[24]

The *History of the World* is no more food for the rapid reader than John Ruskin's *Modern Painters* is; but one can hardly dip for as much as half an hour into its amber translucences without bringing up an idea or an image that will haunt the imagination. The eleventh section of the first chapter deals with one of the main hinges on which Elizabethan thinking turned: "Of Fate; and that the Stars have great influence: and that their operations may diversely be prevented or furthered."

And if we cannot deny [so Ralegh reasons] but that God hath given virtues to springs and fountains, to cold earth, to plants and stones, minerals, and to the excremental parts of the basest living creatures, why should we rob the beautiful stars of their working powers? For seeing they are many in number, and of eminent beauty and magnitude, we may not think that in the treasury of His wisdom, who is infinite, there can be wanting (even for every star) a peculiar virtue and operation, as every herb, plant, fruit, and flower adorning the face of the earth hath the like. For as these were not created to beautify the earth alone, and to cover and shadow her dusty face, but otherwise for the use of man and beast, to feed them and cure them; so were not those uncountable glorious bodies set in the firmament to no other end than to adorn it, but for instruments and organs of His divine providence, so far as it hath pleased His just will to determine.[25]

24. *Ibid.*, sig. A4ᵛ, A5.
25. *Ibid.*, p. 12.

Yet, though the stars above us may in some sense be held to govern our conditions (as Kent says in *Lear*), it is only by working through our own weaknesses; for, says Ralegh, "that either the stars or the sun have any power over the minds of men immediately, it is absurd to think," and "he that contendeth against those enforcements may easily master or resist them." [26] And, as ever, he vitalizes and illumines his conclusion by a daring poetic simile, to the aptness and profundity of which a deep pathos is added when one remembers that the man writing was at the time the king's prisoner.

Lastly, we ought all to know that God created the stars, as He did the rest of the Universal, whose influences may be called His reserved and unwritten laws. But let us consider how they bind: even as the laws of men do; for although the kings and princes of the world have by their laws decreed that a thief and a murderer shall suffer death; and though their ordinances are daily by judges and magistrates (the stars of kings) executed accordingly, yet these laws do not deprive kings of their natural or religious compassion, or bind them without prerogative to such a severe execution, as that there should be nothing left of liberty to judgment, power, or conscience: the law in his own nature being no other than a deaf tyrant. But seeing that it is otherwise, and that princes (who ought to imitate God in all they can) do sometimes, for causes to themselves known, and by mediation, pardon offences both against others and themselves, it were then impious to take that power and liberty from God Himself which His substitutes enjoy, God being mercy, goodness, and charity itself.[27]

Ralegh's patriotism was bred in his bone and ripened by his experience. For him it was no personal passion simply. The incomparable superiority of English soldiers and sailors, manners and morals, and government were in his

26. *Ibid.*, p. 13.
27. *Ibid.*, p. 14.

view incontrovertible facts to whose truth he had been witness infinite times on land and sea. The Englishman who did not prefer his own country to all others sinned not merely against duty and right feeling. For Ralegh he stood convicted of brutish stupidity as well. There must be little in English prose which compares for controlled passion with the account which he published in 1591 of the last fight of his cousin, Sir Richard Grenville: "A Report of the Truth of the Fight about the Isles of Azores, this last summer, betwixt the Revenge, one of her Majesties Ships, and an Armada of the King of Spain."

It would be almost an impertinence to dwell long upon this work. The whirligig of history has given its truth and its sentiment a renewed validity during the present century. Not only is it one of the best examples of patriotic narrative; it is also a masterpiece of farseeing political philosophy. Ralegh's arraignment of what we should now call the spirit of Pan-Hispanianism—of Spanish diplomacy and propaganda, Spanish ambition for world dominion, and Spanish atrocities—said the last word on these subjects in the sixteenth century. Three hundred and twenty-five years later, with a change of adjective which no reader could fail to make, it became again luminous and decisive.

CONCERNING Ralegh's personal career there is a wealth of anecdote and relatively little established fact. Of his early life in Devonshire, at Oriel College, at the Inns of Court, and in the Huguenot service in France, little is recorded. Tradition has it that he and Sidney were together in Walsingham's house in Paris on the night of the St. Bartholomew Massacre (1572).

The earliest official record of his life in London, discovered by the late Mr. Jeaffreson in the Middlesex Sessions Rolls, is significant of the man, though it deals but indirectly with him. He was already in 1577 keeping boisterous servants at his heels, and taking their part when they got themselves into trouble. A true bill date 16 December, 20 Eliz. (1577), gives a lively sketch of a nocturnal merriment of the day:

At Wenloxbarne Co. Midd. at a place called Mount Mill, about eight p. m. of the night of the said day, Richard Paunsforthe, William Paunsforthe and Giles Harmer, late of London yeomen, with seven unknown disturbers of the peace, refused to obey the orders of the watchers at Mount Mill aforesaid . . . and with their swords drawn threatened the said watchers, calling out to them, "Rascals and drunken slaves come an ye dare and we will be your deaths"; and that afterwards the said Richard Paunsforthe, William Paunsforthe, Giles Harmer and others their companions fled from the said watchers, who, together with Anthony Howson the constable of Wenlox Barne, pursued them for the purpose of arresting them, whereupon the same disturbers of the peace with swords drawn assaulted the same watchers, and so handled Anthony Howson that his life was despaired of, and then withdrew to the house of Clement Rigges yeoman.[28]

The disturbing Pauncefords, it turned out, were servants of Walter Ralegh, and the sequel to the liberties they allowed themselves with Anthony Howson's person was Ralegh's appearance before the Justice of the Peace. He is here referred to as "Walter Rawley of Islyngton co. Midd. esq." and as "Walter Rawley esq. of the Court."

Two Middlesex court documents of later years deal with burglaries which the well known gorgeousness of Ralegh's apparel naturally invited.

26 April, 26 Eliz. 1584. At Westminster, Hugh Pewe "late of London gentleman (*sic*) stole a jewel worth eighty pounds, a hat band of pearls worth thirty pounds, and five yards of

28. J. C. Jeaffreson, *Middlesex County Records*, I, 110.

white silk called damask worth three pounds, of the goods and chattels of Walter Rawley, esq."

1 April, 44 Eliz. (1602) two men "broke burglariously into the dwelling-house of Sir Walter Raleighe knt." at St. Martins in the Fields, and stole various articles.[29]

There was much about Ralegh which would attract, either to his profit or his damage, the attention of those who held lightly the sovereignty of the law. There was much likewise to excite the suspicion of the ultraconservative. It is clear that he was, like Marlowe, a brilliant and daring talker, with a dangerous propensity for employing his subtle intelligence in informal argument about religion and politics. In June, 1594, he is said to have sat up all night discussing theology with a condemned Jesuit. Another Jesuit, Father Joseph Cresswell,[30] was appalled by his influence on the young. He speaks of "Sir Walter Raleigh's school of atheism . . . and of the diligence used to get young gentlemen to this school wherein both Moses and our Saviour, the Old and New Testament, are jested at, and the scholars taught among other things to spell God backwards."

The Puritans and the country parsons were no less shocked than the Jesuits. In March, 1594, a commission for causes ecclesiastical was sent to Cerne Abbas in Ralegh's county of Dorset, to administer a formidable interrogatory to various witnesses. The questions were in part:

1. Whom do you know, or have heard to be suspected of Atheism, or Apostacy? . . .

2. Whom do you know, or have heard, that have argued

29. *Ibid.*, pp. 149, 279.
30. I identify this author, who called himself "Philopater," with Cresswell rather than Parsons (as is usually done) on the evidence of Sir Edward Coke at Garnet's trial. Cf. *True & Perfect Relation*, etc. (1606) (S.T.C. 11618), sig. Q1 verso.

or spoken against, or as doubting, the Being of any God? or what or where God is? And to sweare by God, adding, if there be a God, or such like . . . ?

A long list of church wardens, curates, and parsons testified—chiefly one Ralph Ironside, minister of Winterborne, whose name has a Cromwellian ring, and who offered a "Relation of the Disputation had at Sir George Trenchard's table between Sir Walter Raleigh, M. Carew Raleigh, and M. Ironside . . . written by himself and delivered to the Commissioners upon his Oath."

Wednesday sevennight before the Assizes, summer last, I came to Sir George Trenchard's in the afternoon. . . . There were then with the knights, Sir Walter Ralegh, Sir Ralph Horsey, Mr. Carew Ralegh. . . . Towards the end of supper, some loose speeches of Mr. Carew Ralegh's being gently reproved by Sir Ralph Horsey. . . . Mr. Ralegh demands of me what danger he might incur by such speeches. . . . "Soul," quoth Mr. Carew Ralegh, "what is that?" "Better it were," said I, "that we would be careful how the souls might be saved than to be curious in finding out the essence." And so keeping silence, Sir Walter requests me that for their instruction I would answer to the question that before by his brother was proposed unto me. "I have been" (saith he) "a scholar some time in Oxford; I have answered under a bachelor of art and had talk with divers; yet hitherunto in this point (to wit, what the reasonable soul of man is) have I not by any been resolved."

Ironside replied in highly vague theological phrases, to which Ralegh objected as obscure and intricate.

"Yea but what is this ENS ENTIUM?" saith Sir Walter. I answered, "It is God," and being disliked as before, Sir Walter wished that grace might be said, "for that," quoth he, "is better than this disputation." [31]

    31. Professor G. B. Harrison has recently printed all the papers in this case in Appendix 3 of his edition of *Willobie his Avisa*.

Nothing definite seems to have come of the inquiry at Cerne. Ralegh was in 1594 too large a game for the toils which might safely be set for Marlowe and for Kyd, and the deposers in his case lacked temerity to press their charges. Pusillanimous as it is, their testimony gives us our clearest glimpse of Ralegh's mind as it exhibited itself in conversation. Here evidently the wasplike sting of the lyrics and the bold speculative wisdom of the *History of the World* were combined with an incessant intellectual curiosity that drove him to suck the brains of all he met.

THE great task of Elizabethan romanticism was to expand the world in which men live—the world of the senses and the world of the spirit. Imagination and courage are the striking qualities of the four chief leaders of the movement. In these qualities Ralegh was certainly not the least. The fortunes of his life register the rise and decline of the Elizabethan spirit, for of Ralegh is true the precise converse of Macaulay's famous estimate of Bacon: "Whom the wise Queen Elizabeth distrusted and the foolish King James honored and advanced."

Much as Ralegh resembled Sidney and Spenser, he resembled Marlowe more. Marlowe was a dozen years the younger, and he quite lacked the patriotic ardor which was so flaming in Ralegh, Sidney, and Spenser. But otherwise there was a remarkable affinity between the two men. They had perhaps the two most marked individualities of their time. No other Englishman of the sixteenth century displayed so magnificent an appreciation of the marvels of terrestrial exploration; nor did any other before Milton venture so brilliantly into extra-cosmic space. The imagination that executed and described the *Discovery of Guiana* was of the same gorgeous pattern as that which traced the march of Tamburlaine and followed the argosies of Barabas. The "atheism"—which we might now call higher criticism—that framed the teachings of the *History of the World* is of the same brand as that which produced the morality of Doctor Faustus. In Ralegh's "school of atheism" Marlowe seems indeed to have been one of the chief professors, on the evidence of Richard Cholmley, who confessed that he was persuaded by Marlowe's reasons to become an atheist, and "saith and verily believeth that one Marlowe is able to show more sound reasons for Atheism than any divine in England is able to give to prove Divinity, and that Marlowe told him that he hath read the Atheist lecture to Sir Walter Ralegh and others." [32]

That there was a real exchange of ideas between Ralegh and Marlowe is hardly to be doubted. Hariot, whom Kyd names among Marlowe's special friends, is mentioned in the Baines charges against Marlowe as "Sir Walter Ralegh's man," and is again referred to in the Dorsetshire inquiry as one of the preachers of atheism: "one Herriott, attendant on Sir Walter Ralegh, hath been convented before the Lords of the Council for denying the resurrection of the body." This was the man who wrote "A brief and true report of the new found land of Virginia . . . made in English by Thomas Hariot, servant to the above named Sir Walter." When printed at Frankfurt-on-the-Main in 1590, the book was embellished with copper plates illustrating life among the aborigines of America, and by a dedication to Ralegh from the engraver which proves amusingly how far Sir Walter's fame had outtraveled the ability to write good English. "Sir," says the artist,

seeing, that the parte of the Worlde, which is betwene the Florida and the Cap Breton nowe nammed Virginia, to the honneur of yours most souueraine Layde and Queene Eliza-

32. T. Brooke, *Life of Marlowe*, p. 65. "Read the Atheist lecture" is academic terminology for "offered formal instruction in atheism."

BETZ, hath ben discouuerd by yours meanes. And great chardges. And that your Collonye hath been theer established to your great honnor and prayse, and noe lesser proffit vnto the common welth: Yt ys good raison that euery man euertwe [exert?] him selfe for to showe the benefit which they haue receue of yt. Therefore, for my parte I haue been always Desirous for to make yow knowe the good will that I haue to remayne still your most humble saruant. I haue thincke that I cold faynde noe better occasion to declare yt, than taking the paines to cott in copper (the most diligentye and well that wear in my possible to doe) the Figures which do Leuelye represent the forme and maner of the Inhabitants of thesame countrye. . . . Moreouer I haue thincke that the afore said figures wear of greater commendation, If somme Histoire which traitinge of the commodites and fertillitye of the said countrye weare Ioyned with thesame, therefore haue I serue miselfe of the rapport which Thomas Hariot hath lattely sett foorth, and haue causse them booth togither to be printed for to dedicated vnto you, as a thinge which by reigtte dooth allreadye apparteyne vnto you. . . . And soe I comitt you vnto the almyhttie, from Franckfort the fiist of Apprill 1590.

Your most humble seruant
THEODORVS de BRY.

No dweller in the New World can feel cold to Ralegh's achievement or personality. A memorial window in the Church of St. Margaret at Westminster, ennobled by Lowell's lovely quatrain, testifies the fact; and Americans may well take leave of this many-sided genius, with his many foes and many faults, in the terms in which old Thomas Churchyard saluted him upon the publication of the *Discovery of Guiana* in 1596: [33]

A Commendation to all those that either by Invention of Wit, Study of Mind, Travel of Body, Expenses of Purse, or

33. This is the last poem in *Churchyard's Cherishing*, 1596.

Hazard of Life, seeks the Advancement of their Prince and Country.

The world throughout breeds men of sundry kinds,
    Some of great sprite, great skill, and deep engine,
Some mean and base, and some of noble minds,
    Some gross of wit, and some most rare and fine,
As gifts of grace and nature shapes them forth
To show themselves in action men of worth.

    ·   ·   ·   ·   ·   ·   ·

But such that seeks for fame in foreign place,
    Forsakes great ease and wealth where they were bred,
Are special men, and do deserve more grace
    Than all the rest, whatever may be said.

    ·   ·   ·   ·   ·   ·   ·

Then step in place, Sir WALTER RAWLEGH, now,
    Show forth thy face among the worthiest sort.
Thy travel long, thy charge and labor through,
    Crowns thy great pains with praise and good report.
Bid envy blush, for virtue hits the white,
Malice may bark, but hath no power to bite.
World babbles much, but wit doth all behold,
The touchstone must at length try out the gold.
Who reads his book and weighs what he hath done
Shall sound his fame as far as shines the sun.

QUEEN ELIZABETH'S PRAYERS

THE tale of Queen Elizabeth's transactions with the Almighty is long and very characteristic, on the Queen's side at least. She was reared to the sound of prayer, and almost the first literary work of her precocious youth was the translation into Latin, French, and Italian of the popular collection of *Prayers stirring the mind unto heavenly meditations*, which her stepmother and protectress, Queen Katharine Parr, had composed. This was done at the age of twelve; the holograph copy, with the Latin dedicatory letter to her father (dated Dec. 20, 1545), is in the British Museum.[1]

In all the crises of Elizabeth's later life it was natural for her to invoke God in frank and powerful, if often complicated, English. She has left us few more revealing evidences of her style and spirit than these prayers; and it does not detract from their appeal to observe—as I fancy we may in even the latest of them—some persistence of the twelve-year child's confusion between her earthly and heavenly father—the only two powers toward whom she maintained a lasting respect and piety. The God she prays to is a sovereign of wrath and unsearchable ways, who can, however, be counted on to support the Tudor policy and rejoice with his daughter when she outwits her enemies.

The British Museum has a small octavo book, printed

1. Cf. Warner and Gilson, *Catalogue of Western MSS. in the Old Royal and King's Collections*, I (1921), 187. As is well known, Elizabeth had commenced authorship just a year before, with the translation of another work of royal piety, Queen Margaret of Navarre's "Mirror of the Sinful Soul," which she rendered from French verse into English prose and dedicated to Katharine Parr. The holograph of this is in the Bodleian Library and was reproduced in facsimile by P. W. Ames, F.S.A., in 1897.

in 1563, with the title, *Precationes priuatae Reginae E. R.* The contents, divided into *precationes* and *sententiae*, are entirely in Latin and include a long prayer of thanksgiving for restoration of the Queen's health. Two further Latin prayers by Elizabeth are in the *Variae meditationes et preces piae*, printed by Christopher Barker in 1582. There is a copy of this work in the library of Emmanuel College, Cambridge—perhaps the only one extant.[2]

To nearly the same period as Barker's volume of 1582 must belong the delightful manuscript known as "Queen Elizabeth's Prayer Book." It is written on vellum, is three inches high and two wide, and is embellished with miniatures by Nicholas Hilliard of Elizabeth and the Duke of Alençon. It contains six original prayers, the first and last being in English, the others in French, Italian, Latin, and Greek, respectively. This volume was exhibited by Mr. J. W. Whitehead at the Fine Art Society in 1902 and a facsimile produced in forty copies.

Far more could be said in introduction, but I come to the subject of this paper. Two admirable specimens of Queen Elizabeth's prayers are preserved among the Bridgewater Manuscripts in the Huntington Library.[3] One relates to the defeat of the Armada in 1588, the other to the Cadiz voyage of 1596. They have been copied on a single sheet of paper, in a hand and spelling almost crabbed enough to be those of the author herself in her old age. The writing has not been identified. It is not the Queen's, nor is it Sir Thomas Egerton's, but it seems to preserve most of the eccentricities of the original. I shall deal with these documents separately in their contexts.

The Armada prayer requires to be prefaced by another, which was composed at the outbreak of the war with

2. See an article by Miss Ruth Hughey, in *Times Literary Supplement*, Oct. 12, 1933, p. 691.
3. Library mark: 34/C5 (2072, 1205 C).

Spain. I have not seen an early copy of this and quote it in Strype's imperfectly normalized version.[4] It is not certain that the phrasing in this earlier prayer is Elizabeth's—she is referred to in the third person—but it can hardly be doubted that the text received at least her scrutiny and revision:

A prayer used in the queen's chapel, and other places, for preservation, and success against the Spanish navy and forces.

O Lord God, heavenly Father, the Lord of hosts, without whose providence nothing procedeth, and without whose mercy nothing is saved; in whose power ly the hearts of princes, and the end of all their actions; have mercy upon thine afflicted church; and especially regard thy servant Elizabeth, our most excellent queen. To whom thy dispersed flock do fly, in the anguish of their soules, and in the zele of thy trueth. Behold! how the princes of the nations do band themselves against her, because she laboureth to purge thy sanctuary, and that thy holy church may live in security.

Consider, O Lord, how long thy servant hath laboured to them for peace: but how proudly they prepare themselves unto battail. Arise, therefore, maintain thine own cause, and judge thou between her and her enemies. She seeketh not her own honour, but thine; nor the dominions of others, but a just defence of her self; not the shedding of Christian bloud, but the saving of poor afflicted souls. Come down therfore, come down, and deliver thy people by her. To vanquish is all one with thee, by few or by many, by want or by wealth, by weakness or by strength. O! possess the hearts of our enemies with a fear of thy servants. The cause is thine, the enemies thine, the afflicted thine; the honour, victory, and triumph shall be thine.

Consider, Lord, the end of our enterprizes. Be present with

4. J. Strype, *Annals of the Reformation, etc.*, III, Pt. II (1824), 546 f. See *ibid.*, pp. 539–541, for the text of the Latin litanies prepared by the Spaniards for use of those engaged in the conquest of England.

us in our armies. Terrify the hearts of our enemies; and make a joyful peace for thy Christians.

And now, since in this extreme necessity, thou hast put into the heart of thy servant Deborah to provide strength to withstand the pride of Sisera and his adherents, bless thou all her forces by sea and land. Grant all her people one heart, one mind, and one strength, to defend her person, her kingdom, and thy true religion. Give unto all her council and captains wisdom, wariness, and courage; that they may speedily prevent the devices, and valiantly withstand the forces of all our enemies: that the fame of thy gospel may be spread unto the ends of the world. We crave this in thy mercy, O heavenly Father, for the precious death of thy dear Son Jesus Christ. Amen.

Thus Elizabeth took up the sword. The first of the Huntington Library prayers contains her acknowledgments for the victory of 1588, in language authentic and notable enough. The heading is, of course, an addition, presumably by Sir Thomas Egerton. I quote the prayer, for the sake of clarity, in a modernized form and reproduce the actual text in a footnote:

A godly prayer and thanksgiving, worthy the Christian
Debora and Theodosia of our times

Everlasting and omnipotent Creator, Redeemer, and Conserver: When it seemed most fit time to Thy worthy providence to bestow the workmanship of this world or globe, with Thy rare judgment Thou didst divide into four singular parts the form of all this mould, which after time hath termed elements (they all serving to continue in orderly government the whole of all the mass). Which all when, of Thy most singular bounty and never erst-seen care, Thou hast this year made serve for instruments both to daunt our foes and to confound their malice, I most humbly, with bowed heart and bended knees, do render my humblest acknowledgments and lowliest thanks; and not the least for that the weakest sex hath been so fortified by Thy strongest help that neither my people might find lack by my weakness nor foreigners triumph at my ruin.

Such hath been Thy unwonted grace in my days, although Satan hath never made holiday in busy practices both for my life and state. Yet Thy mighty hand hath overspread both with shade of thy blessed wings; so that both neither hath been overthrown nor received shame, but obtained victory to Thy most great glory and their greatest ignominy. For which, Lord, of Thy mere goodness grant us grace to be hourly thankful and ever mindful. And if it may please Thee to pardon my request, give us the continuance in my days of like goodness, that mine eyes never see change of such grace to me, but specially to this my kingdom, which, Lord, grant to flourish many ages after my end. Amen.[5]

5.   a godly prayer & thanck*es* gevyng woorthy the
            Christian Debora & Theodosia of o*ur* dayes

Everlastyng & Oomnypotent Creator Redemer & Conserver when it seemed most fytt tyme to thy woort[h]y provydence to bestowe the woorkmanshipp of this world *or* globe, w*th* thy Rare Iudgment thow dydest devyd in to foure synguler partes, The forme of all this mould, w*ch* after tyme hathe tearmed Elyment*es* they all servyng to contenewe in orde*r*ly gov*er*nment the whole of all the masse, <wytche> wiche all, when of thy most synguler bounty & never earst seene care, thowe hast this yeere mad serve for ynstreweinent*es* boothe to daunt oure foes & to confound theyr mallyce / I most humbly w*th* bowed hart & bended knees,' do Render my humbleyst acknoledgment*es*, and lowlyest thanck*es*, & nott the least, for that the weakest sexe hathe byn so forte-fyed by thy strongest help, y*t* nether my people myght fynd lack by my weaknes nor forrengners tryhumphe at my Ruyn Suche hathe byn th<e>y <w> vnwonted grace in my days althoghe Sathan hathe never mad holy day in bussy practeges boothe for my lyffe & State / Yet y*l* myghty hand hathe overspread bothe w*th* shade of thy blessed wyng*es* / So that boathe nether hathe byn overthrowen nor Receaved shame / But obtayned vyctory to thy moost *grete* glory & theyr greatest ygnomye, for wytche lord of thy meere goodnes grant vs grace to be hourly thanckffull & ever Myndffull, And yf it may pleas the to p*ar*don my Request, gev vs the Contynerans in my dais of lyke goodnes, that myne eyes never see change of suche grace to me But specyally to this my kyngdome / w*ch* Lord grant to ffloryshe many Ag*es* after my end
                                            Amen /

The second prayer on the Bridgewater sheet [6] was written by the Queen when her navy was about to set out, in the summer of 1596, for the attack on Cadiz. There are various contemporary references to this prayer. Thus Camden relates,[7] with regard to the Cadiz expedition, that Elizabeth "appointed a forme of Prayer, whereby they should in euery shippe daily craue *Gods* assistance to their enterprises." And Stow, in the same connection, says: [8]

And in this meane time of all this businesse at Plimmoth, the Queenes Maiestie (well considering that the Lord of hoastes blesseth the hoastes and forces of godly Princes, and giueth victory to the faithfull armies) made a very deuout prayer to Almighty God for the good successe of the fleete, and sent it by Captaine *Edward Conway* to the Generalls, commanding that it should bee dayly said throughout all the Fleete.

Professor G. B. Harrison [9] quotes a letter of the Queen to Essex, at the same time, which I reproduce with Mr. Harrison's preliminary note:

The great expedition to Cadiz, after some weeks spent in training the troops and collecting supplies at Plymouth, after one false start set out on 3rd June. Just before they sailed the Queen sent a prayer, which she had composed for their good success, with the following brief letter:

May 1596

I make this humble bill of requests to Him that all makes and does, that with His benign hand He will shadow you so, as all harm may light beside you, and all that may be best hap to your share; that your return may make you better, and me gladder. Let your companion, my most faithful Charles,[10] be

---

6. This has been rather crowdedly written at the bottom of the same page that contains the Armada prayer, and is in the same hand.
7. *History of Elizabeth* (1630), Bk. IV, p. 91.
8. *Annals* (ed. 1631), p. 772.
9. *The Letters of Queen Elizabeth* (1935), p. 245.
10. Charles, Lord Howard of Effingham, the Lord High Admiral.

sure that his name is not left out in this petition. God bless
you both, as I would be if I were there, which, whether I
wish or not, He alone doth know.

Finally, there is in the Bodleian Library [11] a manuscript
copy of a letter from Richard Fletcher, Bishop of London,
to the Bishop of Lincoln, incorporating a communication
from Whitgift, Archbishop of Canterbury, with respect
to the proposed publication of the prayer. This is as follows:

Prayers for Her Maj^{ties} Navy

After my hearty commendations to your Lordship I have
received Letters from my *Lord's* Grace of Canterburie; and
in them a prayer printed, the tenor of wch Letters is as fol-
loweth. Salutem in Xpo. Your *Lordsh*ip shall receive here
inclosed the forme of a prayer printed, which I think fit to
be sent unto every Bishopp & Custos Spiritualitatis in this
Province with chardge in her Maj^{ties} Name that they give
present order in their severall Jurisdictions, not only for
reverent celebrating and due frequenting in every parish
Church of publique prayers, upon Wednesdays, Fridays,
Sondays & Festivall days, according to the Book of Com*m*on
Prayer but also that this prayer be then & there devoutly
used for the prosperous success and victorious return of her
Maj^{ties} forces and Navie now imployed against the professed
Enemies of her Maj^{tie} & this Kingdom whose malice is kindled
against us for none other cause more than for our main-
tenance of the sincere profession and preaching of Christs
Gospell. Thus commending this to your Godlie care &
speedy *p*erformance I commit your Lord*sh*ip to Gods holy
protection from Lambeth the 3d of June 1596.[12] Your *Lordship's* loving Brother in Christ. Io*hn* Cant.

For the printed prayer there is order given for that her

11. MS. Tanner 77, fol. 88. It is an eighteenth-century copy.
12. The Archbishop appears to have postdated his letter (compare
Fletcher's date at end), perhaps to make it synchronize with the expected date of publication of the printed prayer. He has chanced to hit
upon the actual day on which the expedition sailed from Plymouth.

Maj^ties Printer shall see a competent number of them printed and sent down to your Lordship that every parish within your Dioces may have one of them at the least the price whereof he doth set down unto your Lordship which you must cause to be collected by such your Officers as doth deliver them forth, and to be returned up unto the said Printer in such manner as He shall require your Lordship by his Letters. The necessitie of these times, both for his Heavenly protection of this our Realme, and her Maj^ties Forces assembled for the defence thereof, and the turning awaye of Gods wrath shewed by this unseasonableness of the weather will I hope kindle the heart of every good Minister, both by his own example and by perswasion of his people to a diligent frequenting of publique prayer, according to her Maj^ties tender care, who hath so effectually recommended the same unto us, and therefore your Lordship will I hope be pleased both by your Archdeacons to see the same with all care put in execution. So I recommend your Lordship to his most blessed protection from my Mannor at Fulham, this first of June 1596

                    Yo^r Lordship's loving Bro. in Christ
                              Rich: London
To the Right Revd Father in God
my very good Lorde & Brother the
B. of Lincoln at Buckden give these.
Ex Libro Epistolarum w^i Chaderton Ep^i Linc.

I do not know whether there survives any copy of the printed text to which the bishops refer, but the prayer in question is doubtless the following, as given in the Bridgewater paper. As before, I give it in modernized form and quote the original text in a footnote.[13]

---

13. Strype, *op. cit.*, IV, 302, has a slightly different version, from a Hatfield manuscript, as follows:
    A prayer of queen Elizabeth, upon the going forth of her army
        against the enemy. Found among the lord Burghley's MSS.
Most omnipotent Maker and Guider of all the world's mass, that only searchest and fathomest the bottom of all hearts' conceits, and in them seest the true original of all actions intended: thou that by thy fore-

Her Majesty's privy addition upon this present expedition, when my Lord of Essex was General at the winning of Cales [i.e., Cadiz]

Most omnipotent Maker and Guider of all worlds: Thou only searchest and fathomest the bottom of all hearts, consciences, and conceits, and in them seest the true original of all actions intended. Thou that by Thy foresight dost truly discern * of all actions intended; Thou that by Thy foresight dost truly discern * how no malice of revenge, nor quittance of injury, nor desire of bloodshed, nor greediness of lucre hath bred the resolution of our now set out army; but a heedful care and a wary watch, that no neglect of foes nor our security of harm might breed either danger to us or glory to them: These being grounds, Thou that didst inspire the minds, we humbly beseech Thee with bended knees to prosper the work; and with the best forewind guide the journey, speed the victory, make the return the advancement of Thy glory, the triumph of Thy fame, and surety of this realm, with the least losses of English blood. To this devout petition, Lord, give thy blessed grant. Amen.[14]

---

sight doest truly discern, how no malice of revenge, nor quittance of injury, nor desire of bloodshed, nor greediness of lucre, hath bred the resolution of our new set out army; but a heedful care, and wary watch, that no neglect of foes, nor over-surety of harm, might breed either danger to us, or glory to them. These being the grounds, thou that didst inspire the mind, we humbly beseech thee, with bended knees, prosper the work; and with best forewinds guide the journey, speed the victory, and make the return the advancement of thy glory, the triumph of their fame, and surety to the realm, with the least loss of English blood. To these devout petitions, Lord, give thou thy blessed grant.

W. B. Devereux, *Lives and Letters of the Earls of Essex* (1853), I, 345, prints from an unspecified source a rather mutilated version of the same prayer. (See also note 16 below.)

14. her Ma[ties] prevei adicion vpon this present expedicion when My L of <exse> Essex was generall at the wy[ni]ng of Calse Most omnypotent Maker & gyder of all worldes, Thowe only searcheste & fadomest the bottom of all hartes, Concyences & conceates, and in them seest the true orygenall of all actions entended, Thowe that by thy forsyght doest truly deserne of all <actio> actions entended, Thow that by thy forsight doest truly deserne howe no males of Revenge nor quyttance of Iniurey, nor desyre of Bloudshed, nor gredenes of luker, hathe bredd the Resolucyon of oure nowe sett out armye, But a heed-

It was left to Lord Burghley to phrase the Queen's thanks for the remarkable success at Cadiz. I have not seen the printed "sheet of paper" alluded to below, and so quote the prayer as transcribed by Strype from Burghley's manuscript: [15]

A prayer of thanksgiving for the queen's success against Spain, in the year 1596: composed by the lord treasurer Burghley, July 3. Printed in a sheet of paper. This transcribed from his own MS.

O Lord God of Hosts, everlasting and most merciful Father; we thine unworthy creatures yield unto thy divine Majesty all possible praise and humble thanks for thine infinite benefits, which thou hast of long time plentifully poured upon thine handmaiden and humble servant, our sovereign lady and queen, and upon her whole realm, and us her subjects, the people of this kingdom. And namely, O Lord, for thy gracious respecting us in the merits of thy dear Son our Saviour, and by his interest passing over and forgiving our manifold sins: Thou hast this present summer so favourably conducted the royal navy and army, sent to the seas by our gracious queen, (not for any other worldly respect, but only for the defence of this realm and us thy people, against the mighty preparations of our enemies, threatening our ruin,) by safely directing them unto places appointed, and by strengthening the governors and leaders of the same with counsel and resolution; and blessing them with notable victories, both by sea and land: whereby the insolencies and pride of our enemies, which sought our conquest and sub-

---

ffull care, & a warye watche that no neclecte of foes nor oure securety of harme myght breed ether <del>harme</del> danger to vs, or glorye to them, These beyng growndes, Thow that diddest inspir the Myndes, we humblie beseche the, with bended knees to prosper the work, And wth the best forwynd gyde the Iorney, speede the victory, make the Retorne the advancement of thy glory the tryhumphe of thy fame, And suerty of this Realme, with the least losses of Englyshe bloud, To this devout peticyon lord geve thy blessed graunt   amen.

15. Strype, *op. cit.*, IV, 364–366.

version, is by these late victories daunted, repulsed, and abated.

Grant unto us, most merciful Father, the grace with due thankfulness to acknowledge thy fatherly goodness extended upon us by thy singular favour shewed to thy servant and minister, our sovereign lady and queen. And for thy holy name continue these thy wonderful blessings upon us, to defend us against our enemies, and bless us with thy graceful hand, to the endless praise of thy holy name, and to our lasting joy.

And direct our armies by thy providence and favourable support, to finish these late victories, to the honour of our sovereign, and safety of her realm, that hath most carefully made the same able to overmatch her enemies: so as the noblemen and all others serving in the same navy and army in their charge, may with much honour, triumph, and safety, return home to their countries, annd to give thee due thanks for thy special favour marvellously shewed unto them, in preserving of them all this summer-time from all contagion and mortality by sword or sickness; notwithstanding their force and violence most manfully exercised against their enemies, to the vanquishing great numbers both by sea and land, and to the destruction of their most mighty ships that heretofore have attempted to invade this realm, and of their forts and castles, and waste of their notable substances of their churches, without hurting any persons that did yield, or of any women or children, or religious persons. To whom all favour was shewed that they did require.

All which prosperous successes we do most justly acknowledge, O Lord, to have proceeded from thy special favour. To whom, with thy Son, and the Holy Ghost, be all honour and praise. Amen.

Set forth by authority

In the following year, 1597—the year of the Islands Voyage—the Queen wrote another short prayer, which was prefixed to seven others by different hands and published by the royal printers, "being certain prayers, set forth by authority, to be used for the prosperous success of her majesty's forces and navy." [16] It happens, rather strangely, that a slightly different manuscript copy of this late prayer is found at the end of the same Bodleian Library manuscript that includes Elizabeth's earliest literary work, "The Mirror of the Sinful Soul," of 1544. Thence I quote it *literatim:* [17]

A praier made by her ma^{tie}.

O god the Almaker: keep*er* and guider; The Inverment [i.e., inurement] of thy rare seene vnused and seelde harde of goodnes powered in so ple*n*tifull sorte uppon vs full oft breedes nowe this boldnes to craue with bowed knees and hart*es* of humilitie thy large hands of helpinge power to assiste with wonderfull [?] our iuste cause not founded one prides mocion nor begine [*sic*] on mallice stocke: but thou knowest to whome naught is hid grounded vppon iust defence from wronge <s>: hate, and blinde desier of conquest for such meanes haste thou imp*ar*ted to saue that thou hast given vs by enioyenge such a people as scornes there bludshed where suertie [surely?] oures is one. Fortifie dere god suche hartes in suche sorte as theire best p*ar*te maye be woorste that so the treueste p*ar*te mente woorst with leste losse to such a nacion as despise their lives for there countries good; That all forraine landes may lawde and admiere the omnipotencie of thy works; A facte alone for the onlie to p*er*forme so shall thy name be spred for woonder wraught: and the faithfull incouraged to repose in thine vnfellowed grace and wee that mi*n*de naught but Right incheyned in thy bandes for p*er*petuall service live and die the sacrificers

16. *Ibid.*, pp. 440 f. Strype reprints the 1597 version of the Queen's prayer; it also appears as the last of "Three most excellent Prayers made by the late famous Queene Elizabeth," in Thomas Sorocold's *Supplications of Saints* (1608, etc.). The other two prayers by Elizabeth in Sorocold's collection are textually inferior versions of the two in the Huntington Library.

17. Facsimile, ed. P. W. Ames, fols. 63^{v}, 64.

of our souls for such obtayned favour. Warrante, O lorde, all this with thie comauntiemente.[18]

The foregoing is perhaps the latest of the Queen's special prayers. The Islands Voyage was a considerable fiasco, and if Elizabeth expressed her sentiments on the subject of the Lord, they appear not to have been recorded.[19]

18. The "ti" of this word appears to have been made into a "d," the final reading being "comaundemente."

19. I am indebted to my friend, Captain R. B. Haselden, for material assistance on several points in this paper.

LATIN DRAMA IN RENAISSANCE
ENGLAND *

WHEN that very mundane courtier, Sir John Harington, wrote the *Brief Apology of Poetry and of the Author* which he prefixed to his translation of *Orlando Furioso* in 1591, he found it necessary to remind his readers that dramatic literature was not altogether contemptible, and the examples he thought it prudent to offer were not taken from among the offerings of the vernacular theater but from Latin plays that the universities countenanced: for tragedy "that that was played at St. John's in Cambridge, of Richard III," which he thought "would terrify all tyrannous-minded men from following their foolish ambitions," and for comedies the Cambridge *Pedantius* and the Oxford *Bellum grammaticale*. When he sought to find a London comedy in English to add to these, he was willing to mention but one, "the play of the Cards," and that is one of which we know next to nothing. So, twenty-four years earlier, when John Northbrooke, in his *Treatise* against "vain plays or enterludes" (*ca.* 1577), was swinging the axe of total suppression over the lowly English theater of the 1570's, it was the Latin plays of the age that stayed his arm and forced him to admit that indeed performances might be tolerated "for learning and utterance sake in Latin, and very seldom in English." When the accounts are balanced, it may appear very likely, I think, that it was the Latin plays of England that saved the day for the theater and, so to speak, kept a door open for Marlowe and Shakespeare in that bad third quarter of the sixteenth century, when the old courtly interlude had degenerated into unseemly and ple-

* A paper read at the New England Renaissance Conference in 1940.

beian drivel and a militant puritanism was embattled against all the arts.

The Latin plays, and almost only they, kept a current of ideas in circulation from ancient and contemporary Europe. "The tragedies of Buchanan," Sidney said in his *Apology*, "do justly bring forth a divine admiration," at a time when Sidney found little to admire on the English stage. He should have been thinking not only of Buchanan's two great original tragedies, *Jephthes* and *Baptistes*, but also of Buchanan's Latin versions of the *Medea* and *Alcestis*, by which he had made Euripides readable and actable throughout Europe.

The universities and the Inns of Court were the cradles of modern English drama, and Latin was for them a more practical as well as a more presentable language than English. Queen Elizabeth enjoyed drama in any tongue, and when the great plague of 1592 had paralyzed London, her vice-chamberlain wrote to Cambridge and to Oxford asking that a comedy in English be prepared, to be acted before the Queen at Christmas because "her Majesty's own servants in this time of infection may not disport her Highness with their wonted and ordinary pastimes." The Cambridge reply is extant, addressed to their chancellor, Lord Burleigh.[1] "English comedies," they say, "for that we never used any, we presently have none." They plead the unwillingness of their actors to play in English and request that, if a play must be given, they may either have it acted in Latin or have a longer time for the preparation of an English one, "having no practice," as they scornfully repeat, "in this English vein."

These Latin plays were, indeed, the steppingstones by which professional English drama slowly raised itself out of the bog into which the interlude had fallen. You may read through Polonius' list of "tragedy, comedy, history,

1. F. S. Boas, *University Drama in the Tudor Age*, p. 323.

pastoral, pastoral-comical," etc., with Mr. Harbage's useful census of Anglo-Latin plays (*PMLA*, June, 1938) in hand and pick out the Latin exemplars of each type, appearing in full development ten, twenty, and sometimes fifty years before the earliest vernacular effort in the same kind. For romantic tragedy there is Grimald's suave and poignant *Archipropheta*, acted at Oxford in 1547, or Christopherson's *Jephte* (in Greek) at Cambridge even a little earlier, and there is nothing like them on the English stage till one comes to Peele's *David and Bethsabe* in the late 1580's. The *fons et origo* of the chronicle history play is Legge's *Richardus Tertius* (1579); the first example of romantic comedy out of Boccaccio, the Cambridge *Hymenaeus* of the same year; the earliest elaborate personal satire in dramatic form (since Skelton's *Magnificence* at least) is the Latin *Pedantius* against Gabriel Harvey (Cambridge, 1581). Finally, one can judge of the greater sophistication of the academic theater by comparing two comedies adapted from the same Italian original: Fraunce's Latin *Victoria*, acted at Cambridge in 1579–80, and Munday's *Two Italian Gentlemen*, performed in English before the Queen about five years later.

The Latin plays had form, dignity, and intellectual wit at a time when the vernacular plays very piteously lacked these things, except perhaps in the work of Lyly, who had carefully modeled himself upon the university theater. I want to illustrate these generalities by a brief comment on the best university dramatist contemporary with Lyly, William Gager, whose plays were produced between 1582 and 1593.[2] They dispel a good many false assumptions about his drama. In the first place the Anglo-Latin plays at their best were by no means cold copies of antiquity.

2. *Meleager*, acted 1582, published 1592; *Dido*, acted 1583, MS. at Christ Church, Oxford (Wake supra G. 51); *Rivales*, acted 1583, now lost; *Ulysses Redux*, acted 1592, printed 1592.

Gager's plays are twice as long as the average of Seneca and four times as full of variety and bustle. Even when he was only preparing the Senecan *Hippolytus* for production at Oxford, he found it desirable to expand the play by writing new scenes to please the Elizabethan taste, scenes that shocked the ultrarighteous of his time and would have made the ancient Roman gasp.[3] One is an idyll in which a water nymph makes shameless love to the hero; another brings in Pandarus—no less a solvent of austerity than he—with quite Chaucerian urbanity and with a letter from Phaedra. Thus Pandarus greets the prim young man:

Greetings, Hippolytus, you who shine in country life, and even better in the city! May Diana ever graciously assist your undertakings and every wood furnish you an abundance of beasts to wound . . . May the nymphs (though you are said too austerely to hate the sex) bring you beverage to quench your thirst.

Phaedra's letter also, in the sauciest of elegiacs, is worth translating:

From one whose heart is fixed to you comes health,
    If she can send perhaps what lately lacked her.
Inquire not who I am; shame twice forbids
    To add my name, which is no needful factor.
I'd not be known to you (what good were that?)
    Until I have some small hope of success.
Read you? Or does your prudery prevent?
    Nay, read! This letter's from your friend, no less.

If Gager's respect for what the neoclassicists called decorum had been in any wise comparable with the chaste correctness of his Latin style there would be less reason to read him today and the stage he wrote for would have had less influence; but it was not so. He made the Senecan vehicle convey a kind of dramatic entertainment that is

3. Printed as an appendix to Gager's *Meleager*. Excerpts and discussion will be found in Boas, *op. cit.*, pp. 197–201.

essentially Elizabethan and Gothic. His first play, *Meleager*, is a sultry tragedy of love and hate that crowds the stage with about as much obstreperous action and violent death as *Romeo and Juliet* or *Hamlet*. His last play, *Ulysses Redux*, is a great tragicomic melodrama based upon the *Odyssey* in which every opportunity of excitement, from the boxing match with Irus to the wholesale slaughter of the suitors is exploited for all that it is worth.

But along with the hullabaloo on the stage, in which the Latin drama could almost equal Kyd, there was a graciousness and melody of verse which I think was only approached in one English play before Marlowe. Gager's are crowded with choral songs and inserted lyrics; and these performances in the quantitative meters are so various and delightful that they may help to explain why even Spenser and Sidney doubted in the 1580's whether English prosody was not wholly on the wrong road and should not reform itself on Latin lines. I want to conclude by trying to illustrate a few of the lyric effects which this drama could obtain.

Dido, Chorus at end of Act I (Sapphic strophe)

> Nox diem, solem nebulae reducunt,
> Laeta succedunt ubi dura cedunt;
> Heu fuit clamor pelagi, sed intus
>   Io triumphat.

Night restores day, clouds give us back the sunshine;
Pleasures come fast, following hardships ended.
Ocean's din wrought woe to you: listen how here
    Joy is resounding!

Dido, Chorus at end of Act III (anapestic dimeter)

> O quam velox est fama malum,
> Celeri versans mobilitate!
> Improba vires auget eundo;

> Primo semper parva timore,
> Postea sese tollit in auras,
> Graditurque solo, mox caput inter
>   Nubila condit.

> O what a swift disease is rumor,
> Whirling itself, ay, rapidly changing!
> As it progresses, stronger its force grows.
> Always at first little we dread it;
> Afterward high it mounts in the heavens,
> And it walks on the earth presently with its
>   Head in the cloud banks.

Meleager, Song of the hunters in Act III (Sapphic strophe)

> Publicum, cives, celebrate festum;
> Occidit frendens aper, ecce torvi
> Oris et tergi spolium cruentum:
> Victimas aris date, thura flammis:
> Tota deducat Calydon superbum
>   Laeta triumphum.

> Citizens, let this be a public feast day!
> Dead the gnashing boar! For behold the reeking
> Trophies, grim head, hide, of the monster! Now let
> Altars smoke with myrrh and the chosen victims.
> Calydon may now with rejoicing hold a
>   High-hearted triumph.

> O diem laetum peragant coloni,
> Tuta iam canas segetes aristis
> Proferat tellus, onerata vitis
> Pampinos fundat gravidos racemis;
> Tota deducat Calydon superbum
>   Laeta triumphum.

> Let the husbandmen all the day make merry,
> Let the rescued land now display her harvests,
> Barley bearded-gray, and the laden vine stalks
> Give out branches filled with the heavy clusters.

Calydon may now with rejoicing hold a
    High-hearted triumph.

Turba pastorum celebret choreas,
Fronde velentur iuvenes senesque,
Nulla iam pestis pecori minatur,
Pascuis gramen sine strage carpat;
Tota deducat Calydon superbum
    Laeta triumphum.

Let the shepherd band undertake their dances,
Let the men and youths be entwined with garlands;
No destroyer now is among the cattle,
Now without attack they can graze in the meadows.
Calydon may now with rejoicing hold a
    High hearted triumph.

Meleager, Concluding chorus (iambic dimeter)

Reges timete numina,
Cavete divos temnere.
Maiora nunquam Caelites
Exempla Dii mortalibus
Dedere nobis, quam graves
Poenae suberbis imminent.

Be fearful, Kings, of wills above,
Be loath to flout gods' chastisements.
The heaven-dwellers never gave
Us mortals proofs more powerful
That retribution still impends
(How heavily!) when we are proud.

Ulysses Redux, Last chorus (minor Asclepiadean)

Longos Dulichii ter ducis ambias
Errores pelago, ter quoque Nestoris
Annos praetereas, nec tamen uspiam
Constanti invenias Pennelopae parem;
Tam perrara avis est faemina castior.
Ast error minimus, qui nimius tamen,

Atque aetas brevior, quam Paridis fuit,
Infames Helenae quot similes dabit?
Tam vulgata avis est faemina turpior.
Ecce una misere coniuge pro bona,
Effusus iuvenum nobilis est cruor;
Ecce una misere coniuge pro mala,
Arserunt Phrygii moenia Pergami;
Ergo si noceat, seu mala seu bona,
Nos utroque Deus liberet a malo.

Vivet Penelopes post sua funera
Ingens perpetuo gloria nomine,
Excedetque senis tempora Nestoris;
Pluresque invenias Penelopae pares;
Tam vulgata avis est faemina castior.
Sancte iam videas vivere faeminas,
Aetasque absimiles nostra Helenae tulit,
Quae quondam Paridi rapta Phrygi fuit;
Tam perrara avis est faemina turpior.
Extinxit rabies Dulichii ducis,
Non uxor iuvenes optima nobiles;
Nec tam forma Helenae, quam Paridis furor,
Antiquum Priami diruit Ilium.
Ergo si noceat nec bona nec mala,
Nos utroque Deus quaeso beet bono.

The long sea-wanderings of our chief
You may three times retrace, and thrice
Live Nestor's years, and yet not find
An equal to Penelope:
A chaste dame is so rare a bird.
But shortest travel (though too long)
And briefer life than Paris'
Will discover many Helens:
Bad women are such common fowl.
Behold, for one good wife, alas,
The blood of noble youths was shed!
Behold, for one bad wife, alas,

The walls of Phrygian Troy were burned!
So if she harm, though bad or good,
God keep us free from either ill.

Penelope's great fame will live
After her death with lasting praise,
And will exceed old Nestor's age;
And you may find a number like her,
Good women are such common fowl.
For now you may see wives live chastely;
Our age has borne them unlike Helen,
Who was once raped by Phrygian Paris:
A wicked woman's a rare bird.
Ulysses' wrath, not his choice wife,
Was what destroyed the noble youths;
Less Helen's charms than Paris' rage
Demolished Priam's ancient Troy.
So if she harm not, good or bad,
God bless us, pray, with either boon.

WILLOBIE'S *AVISA*

I OFFER this paper as an appendix to the edition of Shakespeare's *Poems* which Professor Feuillerat prepared for the *Yale Shakespeare* in 1927, in the hope that it may possess a little of the same good sense.

OF the poems which followed the lead of Shakespeare's *Venus and Adonis* and *Lucrece*, none came so near rivaling them in popularity, and none invites so much critical attention today, as *Willobie his Avisa*, "or the true picture of a modest maid and of a chaste and constant wife," which appeared first in 1594 (entered on the Stationers' Register, September 3), and reached at least its sixth edition in 1635. All of the extant copies contain prefatory epistles signed by "Hadrian Dorrell," who describes himself as a student of Oxford and imputes the authorship of the poem to his "very good friend and chamber fellow, M. Henry Willobie." Two sets of commendatory verses, with veiled signatures, make the same ascription, one of them conferring a kind of immortality upon Willobie's book by incorporating the earliest known literary reference to *The Rape of Lucrece*, which had been registered less than four months before (May 9, 1594):

> Yet Tarquin pluck'd his glistening grape,
> And Shake-speare paints poor Lucrece' rape.

The urge to exploit this obviously riddling production in the interest of Shakespearean biography has beset several generations of critics, and has in recent years—to say naught of wilder endeavors—inspired two most learned and ingenious, though mutually inconsistent, interpretations. Professor G. B. Harrison's *Essay*, appended to his excellent edition of the poem (*Bodley Head Quartos,*

1926), tentatively follows the late Arthur Acheson in assigning the authorship to Matthew Roydon, known as a member of the Ralegh-Marlowe-Chapman group of "atheists," the so-called "School of Night." In the light of the depositions taken against Ralegh and his circle at Cerne Abbas, Dorsetshire, in March, 1594, Mr. Harrison would explain the *Avisa* as a lampoon on Ralegh's enemies, including Sir Ralph Horsey and, in minor degree, Shakespeare and the Earl of Southampton.

On the other hand, Professor Leslie Hotson, in an interesting chapter of his *I, William Shakespeare* (1938, pp. 53–70), finds new documentary reason to confirm the authorship of Henry Willobie, and points to biographical links which might indicate an acquaintance through Shakespeare's friend, Thomas Russell, between Willobie and the greater poet. By this reading, the poem's attitude to Shakespeare is admiring rather than satiric, and it has no connection with the "School of Night," nor with Southampton and the *Sonnets*. Such seems to me the more probable view, and I believe it still possible to throw a little light upon *Willobie his Avisa* by analyzing the explanatory material which the early editions contain.

Previous theories have been handicapped by the fact that they have depended exclusively upon the first edition of the poem (1594) and the last (1635), since these were the only ones accessible in English public libraries. Of the second edition, which certainly was printed in 1596, and the third, which probably followed in 1599, I know no extant copy; but the Harvard Library has the fourth edition of 1605 and the Huntington Library has the fifth of 1609, and these enable us to correct certain points which have been inaccurately presented in the late text of 1635, or faultily deduced from it. (All the four known editions of this work are in the Folger Library, but at present unavailable for study.)

OF Henry Willobie, the avowed author of the poem, certain facts have long been known, and Mr. Hotson has added valuable details. He was about eleven years younger than Shakespeare, and was the second son of an important Wiltshire gentleman, who resided at West Knoyle, a couple of miles from the boundary of Dorsetshire. He matriculated from St. John's, Oxford—as a "commoner" or independent member—on December 10, 1591, at the age of sixteen, and took his B.A. degree, as a member of Exeter College, February 28, 1594–95, five months after "Hadrian Dorrell" had reported of him that, "being desirous to see the fashions of other countries for a time," he had "departed voluntarily to her Majesty's service." This, as Mr. Hotson says, suggests a doubt of Dorrell's *bona fides;* though I do not know that there is anything absolutely incredible in a wealthy commoner's allowing himself an interval abroad, and still, as we say, graduating with his class. The fact that he shifted colleges between matriculation and graduation might be relevant to this matter.

Willobie's repute as a poet had spread so far by 1595 that the Cambridge author of *Polimanteia,* William Covell, selected his name for mention among the sweet singers of Oxford. That, of course, proves no more than the immediate popularity of the *Avisa;* but Dorrell insists that Willobie had much other verse in manuscript, including a poem on Susanna not now known. Mr. Hotson has discovered a legal document which shows our Henry Willobie to have been still alive in August, 1597; but the 1605 edition of the *Avisa* adds a new poem, "The Victory of English Chastity," "never before published," and signed by Thomas Willobie, "Frater Henrici Willoby nuper defuncti." Since Henry did have a younger brother, Thomas, this supports the identification of the poet; and if there is truth in the 1605 title-page assertion, i.e., if the added poem was not found in the earlier lost editions, it should prove that Henry Willobie, author of *Avisa*, died shortly before 1605.

"Hadrian Dorrell," the editor of the poem, announces himself as Willobie's chamber fellow, hence, one would suppose, a member of either St. John's or Exeter College, and he signs two prefaces from Oxford on October 1, 1594, and June 30, 1596, respectively; but the Oxford records know nothing of such a person. Thomas Darrell, indeed, the son of a Berkshire clergyman, matriculated, as from Brasenose College, on the same day as Willobie (Dec. 10, 1591), but there is no Hadrian. According to Clark's *Register*, the name Adrian or Hadrian was borne, during the decade concerned, by only three or four quite impossible Oxonians. We are left, therefore, with the alternatives: Either (1) "Hadrian Dorrell" is a yet undeciphered pseudonym or anagram for Willobie's actual chamber fellow; or (2) it is a name invented by Willobie, who, under cover of it, wrote the prefaces himself. The second is perhaps the more likely, though there is no indication that Willobie was at Oxford at the date of the later preface, that is, sixteen months after he had been admitted to his degree. Moreover, if he wrote "Dorrell's" earlier preface, announcing his own absence in foreign parts, the hoax would have been obvious to all his Oxford friends; but this would hardly have been out of keeping with the current conventions of authorship.

WE may now consider the poem itself. It appears that Henry Willobie, an Oxford undergraduate aged about eighteen, was moved by the publication of *Venus and Adonis* to write an amatory, but moral, poem of his own. So I understand the statement in his second stanza:

> My sleepy muse that wakes but now,
> Nor now had wak'd if one [i.e., Shakespeare] had slept,
> To virtue's praise hath pass'd her vow.

He may have had some knowledge of Shakespeare through mutual acquaintances, and in that case might possibly have heard something of the latter's *Lucrece*. It would have been impossible for him to compose the three thousand lines of *Avisa* in the short interval after *Lucrece* had appeared in print, but that event occurred in time to permit a reference to it in one of the prefatory poems.

Willobie adopted the well-known rime scheme of *Venus and Adonis*, but he secured a faster movement by cutting the five-foot meter to four feet, throwing the narrative more conspicuously into dialogue, and organizing the poem in short "cantos." The last deviation may have been suggested by the symmetry of Spenser's "Tears of the Muses" and "Daphnaida." Willobie evidently intended units of six six-line stanzas, but has not carried the plan through with Spenserian precision. A more essential novelty was obtained through replacing mythological voluptuousness by the love adventures of a real woman. Avisa, "virtue's bird," must have been to some extent actual—the local hints are so precise. They make it appear that she was born in the general neighborhood of Cerne Abbas, Dorset,

> At wester side of Albion's Isle,
> Where Austin pitch'd his monkish tent.
> (Harrison's ed., p. 23.)

She is the daughter of a poor man, who was "mayor of the town" (p. 27), not Cerne Abbas, but "not far from thence" (p. 26); and is married to the keeper of the George Inn (canto 46, p. 121). She lives at a Crystal Well (twice mentioned, pp. 26, 107) beside

> A rosy vale in pleasant plain (p. 26).

The rosy vale, though I have not been able to identify it, seems to have local significance, for the added poem by

Thomas Willobie refers to the same place in describing his hero (p. 246):

> A noble prince in *Rosie* born,
> *Rogero* hight.

The description of Avisa's surroundings in the first canto agrees very well with the topography of northern Dorsetshire; e.g. (p. 27),

> Along this plain there lies a down,
> Where shepherds feed their frisking flock;

and the scene is more definitely fixed by an apparent reference to Sherborne Castle as lying to the east (p. 26):

> At east of this a castle stands,
> By ancient shepherds [i.e., bishops] built of old,
> And lately was in shepherd's hands,
> Though now by brothers bought and sold [i.e., exploited].

The brothers I take to be the Ralegh brothers, Walter and Carew, who had supplanted the Bishops of Salisbury at Sherborne in 1592. On such grounds, tested by a personal visit to the region, Mr. Harrison decides upon Sherborne town as Avisa's residence. Yeovil in Somerset, a half-dozen miles farther west, might suit as well. The distance from Willobie's home at West Knoyle would be about twenty miles.

WILLOBIE's verse is flat and boyishly immature, but it has the liveliness that often comes from authentic details; and a reputation for piquant topicality is the only thing that could understandably have kept this monotonous narrative of the chaste Avisa in demand through six editions and forty years. It is the only thing also which would seem to explain the fact that so heavily moral a poem was ordered "called in," i.e., withdrawn from circulation, by ecclesiastical authority in June, 1599.

With much repetition, but no small energy and some dramatic vividness, Willobie shows Avisa arguing down the successive solicitations of (1) an unnamed nobleman of "riper years," referred to figuratively as "unhappy Lily"; (2) a gentleman called Cavaleiro, with "wanny cheeks" and "shaggy locks," whom Old Dame Experience has made wise, and whom it is indeed tempting to equate with Sir Ralph Horsey, the Lord Lieutenant of Dorsetshire; (3) "D. B., a Frenchman," meaning, according to Dorrell, one who has the Gallic temperament and technique in love. His vain suit is prolonged through five years, and is followed by that of the Anglo-German type, (4) "Dydimus Harco," a man of deceptively "safe and sober cheer," whose name might be translated "Brother Charo," i.e., Carew (Carowe) Ralegh, known in local matters as Sir Walter's *alter ego* and rubber stamp. Fifth is the Spanish-Italian type, who, as Dorrell says, "more furiously invadeth his love and more pathetically endureth than all the rest." This type is personified by young "Henrico Willobego" himself, whose suit is the most ardent of all and is encouraged by his "familiar friend," W. S., the "old player" and expert in love. It may be a personal reference to Shakespeare, or may be only another tribute to the provocative character of *Venus and Adonis*. In this last section of the poem, prose inserts of some length occur, and the handling begins to suggest that of a novel by Greene, even to the fictional conclusion: "H. W. [in ed. 1605, 'Hen. Will.'] was now again stricken so dead that he hath not yet any farder assayed, nor I think ever will; and where [i.e., whether] he be alive or dead I know not, and therefore I leave him." Then follow "The Author's Conclusion" in the usual meter, summarizing Avisa's virtues, and saying that a great deal more might be spoken of her, and finally two short poems in different style, which do not directly mention Avisa but laud her special attributes, constancy and content.

ONE is likely to get the impression that an Elizabethan youth could write a long poem on nearly any subject with the greatest ease and nonchalance, but was then driven into paroxysms of nervousness, and into the weirdest freaks of fancy, when devising an excuse for its publication. Henry Willobie was moved to call in, or invent, "Hadrian Dorrell," who prefaced the first edition of *Avisa* with two letters. The first, addressed "To all the constant ladies and gentlewomen of England that fear God," apologizes for depriving them of a defense of their constant chastities which Dorrell has long since promised to some of them. He admits that the present occasion, "publishing now the praise of a constant wife," would have been most fit for the publication also of Dorrell's work, "if I had been but almost ready." But he must leave the performance of that task to some later time. A modern reader detects no disingenuousness in this letter. It is disillusioning that Dorrell's defense of the ladies never appeared, nor anything else by him, and that so Argus-eyed a searcher of records as Professor Mark Eccles can find "no reason to credit the reality of Hadrian Dorrell."

Dorrell's second letter, "To the gentle and courteous reader," is much longer and hardly less plausible. He publishes his absent friend's poem without the latter's authority, and he knows nothing of the meaning of it. He must leave the reader to decide whether it "be altogether feigned, or in some part true, or altogether true and yet in most part poetically shadowed." He offers the reader fallacious assistance by citing some good reasons to believe *Avisa* "altogether a feigned matter, both for the names and the substance," and then giving better reasons to think "something of truth hidden under this shadow." A contemporary reader would end with the impression that the incidents rest on truth, and a modern critic with the conclusion that Willobie-Dorrell wishes to eat the cake of sensational authorship without the consequent pains of *scandalum magnatum*.

Willobie his Avisa would doubtless have gone its dubious way, without further enlightenment of posterity, if a certain Peter Colse had not published his *Penelope's Complaint*, "or a mirror for wanton minions," in direct opposition to it a year and a half later. This work was entered on the Stationers' Register, February 13, 1595–96, and Colse dedicated it to the Lady Edith, wife of Sir Ralph Horsey, calling it "the firstlings of my scholar's crop," and justifying its publication by the fact that "an unknown author hath of late published a pamphlet called *Avisa*," "a vainglorious Avisa," he says later, "seeking by slander of her superiors to eternize her folly." The 218 six-line stanzas, written in confessed imitation of *Avisa*, contain no definite reference to that poem; but some introductory Latin elegiacs by "S. D." (who, so far as I can see, may well have been Samuel Daniel), "Amico suo charissimo P. C.," stress more openly than Colse's prefaces the opposition of Avisa and Penelope. Avisa is "obscura obscuro faemina nata loco," a humble woman born in a humble spot, and furthermore "coniux cauponis, filia pandochei," wife of an innkeeper and daughter of a publican; whereas "Penelope satrapae est coniux illustris," that is, I suppose, the wife of a Lord-Lieutenant. It is to be inferred that the Horsey family resented *Avisa*, and it is possible to conjecture that the matriculation of Peter Coles of Dorset, "son of a plebeian," at Oxford, November 9, 1599, at the late age of twenty-six, may have been by the Horsey's bounty, and may have something to do with their appreciation of the talents and loyalty expressed in *Penelope's Complaint*.

Within about four months Colse's work had called forth the second (lost) edition of *Avisa*, with Hadrian Dorrell's new "Apology, showing the true meaning of *Willobie his Avisa*," dated at Oxford, June 30, 1596. In this excited and incoherent paper, which is largely at variance with his prefaces of two years before, Dorrell hastens to add "a new instruction for such as I understand have made of the other a false and captious construction," especially P. C., "who seemeth to be a scholar," but "hath been carried away with this stream of a misconceived folly." Dorrell is now most plaintive in his assurance "that there is no particular woman in the world, that was either party or privy to any one sentence or word in that book." Moreover, he strangely says, "This poetical fiction was penned by the author at least for thirty and five years sithence," which would seem to mean, based on conditions of a generation earlier, a grossly implausible assertion, but less absurd than the interpretation of some modern critics who assume Dorrell to be stating that the poem was *written* thirty-five years earlier.

Dorrell protests too much, and by his denials makes it clear that Avisa was being understood as an actual woman of similar name, doubtless one of the many Avices whom the church registers of the district record. "If any man, therefore, by this should take occasion to surmise that the Author meant to note any woman, whose name sounds something like that name, it is too childish and too absurd, and not beseeming any deep judgment, considering there are many things which cannot be applied to any woman." He also implies that Peter Colse thought he knew what men were figured in Avisa's suitors, though Colse has not himself suggested this. "But to conclude," says Dorrell, "thus much I dare precisely avouch, that the Author intended in this discourse neither the description nor praise of any particular woman, nor the naming or cyphering of any particular man . . . and therefore this P. C. hath offered manifest injury to some, whatever they be, whom his private fancy hath secretly framed in conceit."

My quotations, though modernized in spelling, are from the 1605 edition, the earliest extant one containing this letter. The editions of 1609 and 1635 have many typographical variations (e.g., the date "1569" for "1596" in ed. 1635) but no essential additions or omissions. With one exception, I see no reason to suppose that the letter did not appear in the edition of 1596 virtually as we have it. Dorrell's concluding paragraph, however, invites a question. It runs, in the texts of 1605 and later: "This is the least that I could say, and the last that ever I will say touching this matter in defence of my friend. If any notwithstanding will continue the error of their unsatisfied minds, they must forever rest in the rightless erring, till the Author (*now of late gone to God*) return *from Heaven* to satisfy them farder touching his meaning. And so farewell. Oxford this 30. of June, 1596." If Dorrell wrote in 1596 the words I have italicized, he stands convicted by Professor Hotson of an inartistic mendacity. I venture to register the wager that, when a copy of the 1596 quarto is discovered, it will be found to read simply: "till the Author return to satisfy them farder touching his meaning." The italicized words could have been naturally added by the publisher in 1605, or at any other date after Willobie's death.

There is one slight point which an ultra-clever criticism might cite as throwing doubt on Henry Willobie's actual authorship of the poem. In the letter just discussed, Dorrell upbraids P. C. for calling the poet of *Avisa* "unknown." "The author was unknown [gibes Dorrell], not because he [i.e., Colse] could not, but because he would not, know him; his true name being open in every page." The meaning is that Willobie's name occurs in the title of the work and consequently on all the headlines of the book. Now, it might be urged, if Willobie were the unrecorded figure, and Dorrell the actual Oxford poet, it would be easier to accommodate this statement with the obvious prudential purposes of the letter; but, since the facts are just otherwise, the mythical Dorrell ought not to be directing suspicion to the real Willobie. If there is force in such a view, the answer, I suppose, is that this particular slur at P. C.'s stupidity, occurring in a series of such, was too good to be left out, and can be further accounted for by the vanity of authorship. At all events, it seems to assert a truth in stating that this poem is properly known as "Willobie's *Avisa*."

CHRISTOPHER MARLOWE

OW-A-DAYS every shoemaker's son must be sent to school and every beggar's brat study his books, come to be a writer, dwell with a lord or falsely be a friar and serve the fiend. So that, instead of the beggar's brat we shall have a bishop [i.e., poet] who will sit close to the peers of the land. And the sons of lords will bow low to these rascals and knights will crouch and scrape to them. And their fathers were shoemakers, soiled with grease, and their teeth jagged as a saw from working with leather." [1]

GIVEN the usual university training, a free field and no favor, and six years more to live, what can a man of twenty-three do with his life? The answer to this question which Christopher Marlowe's performances between 1587 and 1593 stamped upon the records of time may well arouse pride in those who stand about the point in years where the poet's genius first broke into meteoric flame. For the rest of us, already declined beyond where the meteor dropped full-blazing beneath our horizon, the thought may bring more of humiliation; but for all it must bring wonder and the high exaltation man feels in the triumphs of man.

> Thou canst not hit it, hit it, hit it;
> Thou canst not hit it, my good man.

Thus, in the words of one of Shakespeare's frivolous young ladies, the Way of the World teases us all with the

1. *Piers the Plowman's Creed* (*ca.* 1394), ll. 744 ff., translated by Prof. A. R. Benham, *English Literature from Widsith to the Death of Chaucer*, p. 391.

bauble fame. Well for us if we can find in Marlowe and
his like the consolation Boyet found:

> An I cannot, cannot, cannot;
> An I cannot, another can!

> Art is long and time is fleeting.

> Ars longa, vita brevis.

> The lyf so short, the craft so long to lerne.

So in a dozen languages have men complained of "Time,
that subtle thief of youth," but the complaint is hardly
justified, for the finest art has often outstripped time. A
half-dozen years sufficed Shakespeare for his greatest tragedies, three or four were enough for Coleridge, some three
for Keats, and one for Chatterton. Viewed in this light,
time is leaden-footed indeed beside the fairy speed of art,
and length of days becomes a sheer irrelevance.

And though Marlowe died with his youth still full upon
him, he takes his stand among poets as a full-grown man,
a finished and accomplished force. In one of the last of all
his writings (*Fortnightly Review*, May, 1916), Swinburne very eloquently [2] stated this fact:

"Marlowe differs from such little people [as Greene
and Peele] not in degree, but in kind; not as an eagle differs
from wrens or tit-mice, but as an eagle differs from frogs
or tadpoles. He first, and he alone, gave wings to English
poetry; he first brought into its serene and radiant atmosphere the new strange element of sublimity. And, innova-
tor as he was, revolutionist and creator, he was no less
loyal, no less competent an artist, no less perfect and in-
stinctive a workman in words than Chaucer or than Spenser was before him. He had neither the boyish humour
nor the childish pathos of Chaucer; he had nothing of

2. And not without Swinburnian exaggeration.

Spenser's incomparable melody and all-but-inexhaustible fancy; but among all English poets he was the first full-grown man."

"Souls of poets dead and gone" continue to speak to the world through two media: by their achievements and their character. Though never altogether distinct, the two voices cannot be wholly merged, and it may profit to consider in each of these manifestations the translunary soul of Marlowe.

It was Ben Jonson, than whom England has produced few finer critics, who characterized with immortal felicity the first of the Cambridge scholar's achievements: "Marlowe's mighty line."

Unriming decasyllables had been written before Marlowe by several sixteenth-century Englishmen: by the Earl of Surrey and Nicholas Grimald, by Sackville and Norton in *Gorboduc*, by Gascoigne in *The Steel Glass*, by Peele in *The Arraignment of Paris*. Various purposes seem to have prompted these innovators: the desire to approximate the Latin hexameter in the case of Surrey, or the senarius of Seneca in *Gorboduc*, the desire for a prose-like vehicle of contemporary satire in Gascoigne, the effort at classic elegance in the play of Peele. These were all rather prosaic ambitions, and except in Peele's case, they led to prosaic effects. It was Marlowe who changed the sow's ear into the silken purse, who transformed the homely tool of the translators and satirists and dialogue makers into the divinest instrument of romantic passion. When Marlowe employed it, blank verse became at once what Shakespeare, Milton, Tennyson have again and again proved that it can hardly cease to be: the grandest and most expressive of all English meters.

Few poets, certainly, have paralleled the ability which Marlowe shows in his early plays of condensing an entire lyric into a single glorious verse. In *Tamburlaine* and

Faustus particularly, the splendid scenes as they unroll display mighty lines which glitter and writhe like burnished living serpents. Sometimes the reader is shaken into breathlessness by ten syllables that reveal the wild strange beauty of a yearning soul:

> Was this the face that launched a thousand ships?
>
> Tis magic, magic, that hath ravished me.
>
> And ride in triumph through Persepolis.
>
> The sweet fruition of an earthly crown.
>
> Still climbing after knowledge infinite.
>
> Infinite riches in a little room.

Sometimes we are startled by the naked revelation of a mind laid bare in the moment of ultimate decision:

> A God is not so glorious as a king.
>
> I'd give them all for Mephistophilis.
>
> And all is dross that is not Helena.

Sometimes the line becomes a paean of exulting arrogance:

> There is no music to a Christian's knell!
>
> Holla, ye pampered jades of Asia!
>
> Have not I made blind Homer sing to me?
>
> I hold the fates bound fast in iron chains.
>
> O girl! O gold! O beauty! O my bliss!

Again it sums up with a divine finality one of the colossal truths of human experience:

> For Tamburlaine, the scourge of God, must die.
>
> Cut is the branch that might have grown full straight.
>
> And where hell is, there must we ever be.

And sometimes the single terrible line illumines as with white flame the soul's last effort against the inevitable:

Break heart, drop blood, and mingle it with tears!
But stay awhile, let me be king till night.
I'll burn my books! Ah, Mephistophilis!

MARLOWE's second achievement was that he first taught the drama what Spenser was teaching verse fiction—the splendor of romance. As the first great romantic dramatist Marlowe taught the difference between living and life, the great idea prerequisite to all appreciation of men and art. Previously, the desultory writers of the age had dealt with the externals of living: uncomfortable living, as in the lovers' pains of Surrey and Wiat; fashionable living, as in Lyly; foolish living, as in Gascoigne's satires; evil living, as in Greene. It remained for Marlowe, as it always does remain for the great romanticist, to throw open the holy of holies and show us life itself. The radiance of his mind burns away the misty externalities and reveals the protoplasmic life within. The smug questions of expediency and crass morality grow impossible. Does Tamburlaine live well or ill? Does Faustus live wisely or unwisely? Does Barabas act justly or unjustly? Who can possibly care for an answer? As well ask whether a mountain ought to tower in sterile grandeur above the pleasant useful meadows, or whether the ocean has a right to roar.

Life's the thing, not how, or where, or why one lives. In some of the most gorgeous and dynamic lines that ever accompanied the apparition of newborn Athene, Marlowe spoke the message of romance:

From jigging veins of riming mother wits
And such conceits as clownage keeps in pay
We'll lead you to the stately tent of war.

The time of homily and dalliance is past; the age of vision is at hand. From this moment the great crusade is on. Excelsior is the motto of every man. The votaries of life burst their manacles, and in the words of the last of Marlowe's Elizabethan followers,

> O'er bog or steep, through strait, rough, dense or rare,
> With head, hands, wings, or feet,[3]

pursue their way.

The avenues through which the chase proceeds are as numerous as the lives of men: regal ambition, knowledge, the sacred hunger for gold, the thirst for friendship, or the consuming fire of love.[4] But always there is life ahead, life which "Wills us to wear ourselves and never rest," and makes us all crusading knights.

> That in conceit bear empires on our spears,
> Affecting thoughts coequal with the clouds.

Is it not a fine, a necessary thing that man should once in a long ago do what Marlowe's figures do—overleap the safe and comfortable bounds of expediency, law, and mortality itself in reckless pursuit of "Those thoughts that wander through eternity?" [5] And it was Milton again who put into the mouth of his most romantic and Marlowesque figure the proper comment upon the careers of Tamburlaine and Faustus, Guise, Barabas and Mortimer:

> That strife
> Was not inglorious, though the event was dire.[6]

This, then, was the second specific achievement of Marlowe, in which he labored, let us not forget, side by side with Spenser, though in a very different—in a dramatic—manner.

Writing before the romantic achievement of either Spenser or Marlowe was performed, Sir Philip Sidney spoke golden words of what was perhaps the finest poem

3. *Paradise Lost*, II, 948 f.
4. *Tamburlaine, Faustus, Jew of Malta, Edward II, Dido.*
5. *Paradise Lost*, II, 148.
6. Satan, *Paradise Lost*, I, 623 f.

of martial romance then audible to English ears: "Certainly, I must confess mine own barbarousness. I never heard the old song of Percy and Douglas, that I found not my heart moved more than with a trumpet; and yet is it sung but by some blind crowder, with no rougher voice than rude style." [7] When the blind crowder is supplanted by Marlowe, "the Muses' darling" as Peele called him, and the rude style undergoes apotheosis into the mighty line, then it is no wonder that romantic poetry works miracles in the mind of man and the ideal poet described by Sidney stands confessed: "He cometh to you with words set in delightful proportion . . . and with a tale, forsooth, he cometh unto you, with a tale which holdeth children from play, and old men from the chimney corner." For three hundred years *Tamburlaine* and *Faustus* have done no less.

MARLOWE's third great achievement was the discovery of the secret of dramatic action. It seems usual to think and write of this poet as a great lyrist, who by pure chance blundered upon the drama in his search of a means of self-expression. We may well doubt whether blunders of this kind happen in the case of men of genius; certainly nothing of the sort happened to Marlowe.

Few men can ever have possessed a surer native sense of dramatic values, and it may very reasonably be questioned whether Shakespeare himself taught English drama much more in the way of technique than Marlowe taught it—whether, that is, Shakespeare was able to improve the stage practice of Marlowe more than Marlowe improved that of his predecessors. It seems clear, in so far as contemporary tributes and allusions permit us to judge, that even the first play, *Tamburlaine*, owed its sweeping success not so much to the splendid poetry of its lines and the roman-

7. *The Apology for Poetry* (ca. 1580).

tic wonder of its story as to the sheer brilliance of its dramatic effects. The instinct for dramatic situation is everywhere apparent, and it was this instinct to which the greatest succeeding dramatists did homage.

In *The Case is Altered*, Ben Jonson offers the flattery of imitation to the effective situation near the opening of the first part, where Tamburlaine, inflamed by the beauty and evident admiration of Zenocrate, lays aside his shepherd dress and dons the complete armor of a knight.

> Tamb.   But tell me, madam, is your grace betroth'd?
> Zen.   I am, my lord,—for so you do import.
> Tamb.   I am a lord, for so my deeds shall prove;
>   And yet a shepherd by my parentage. . . .
>   Lie here, ye weeds, that I disdain to wear!
>   This complete armor and this curtle-axe
>   Are adjuncts more beseeming Tamburlaine.[8]

And Shakespeare makes Pistol recall to us that dramatic visualization of military glory at its zenith, when indeed the conqueror does ride in triumph, "drawn in his chariot by [the kings of] Trebizond and Soria, with bits in their mouths; reins in his left hand, in his right hand a whip with which he scourgeth them." [9]

It is not merely in the portrayal of his chief figures, however, that Marlowe's dramatic eye appears. The great dramatist is revealed in the very first speech of the first play, in those five lean lines of Mycetes, which at once tear the veil from before the gorgeous impotence of the Persian throne, exposing the mental bankruptcy of the sovereign and the crying need for a real man:

> Brother Cosroe, I find myself aggrieved,
> Yet insufficient to express the same,
> For it requires a great and thundering speech.

8. *Tamburlaine*, pp. 228 ff.
9. *Tamburlaine*, IV, iii, S.D.

> Good brother, tell the cause unto my lords;
> I know you have a better wit than I.

The first part of Tamburlaine exhibits in its structure as a whole a certainty of purpose and method no less extraordinary in a playwright's initial work than that expressed in the astounding prologue. The first act pictures the sudden blossoming of the hero's innate ambition under the stimulation of Zenocrate's beauty and the threat of the thousand horsemen of Theridamas. This act ends with the establishment of the moral ascendency of the shepherd over, first, his intended captor Theridamas, and, second, his destined bride.

> Won with thy words and conquered with thy looks,
> I yield myself, my men, and horse to thee,
> To be partaker of thy good or ill,

cries Theridamas. "We yield unto thee, happy Tamburlaine," says the supercilious Agydas; and Zenocrate ends the act with her still reluctant acceptance of the inevitable: "I must be pleased perforce,—wretched Zenocrate."

The second act shows this moral ascendency transmuted into actual achievement, as the shepherd's imagination is fired by the picture of the royal conqueror riding in triumph through Persepolis; and the act concludes with a magnificent finale, as the hero takes the Persian crown and sets it, Napoleon-like, upon his own head:

> So; now it is more surer on my head
> Than if the gods had held a parliament,
> And all pronounced me king of Persia.

The opening of the third act introduces the vainglorious and mighty Bajazet, most redoubtable of all the Scythian's foes, threatening vast ruin to the upstart; and this act rises rapidly to the crisis of the play, the battle of Angora. When the act ends, the King of Persia is the supreme ruler of all Asia:

> Come, bring them in; and for this happy conquest
> Triumph, and solemnize a martial feast.

The fourth act is a structural marvel. The conqueror has apparently reached the height of his career. Is not his boasted fortune now preparing to forsake him? The first scene shows us an ominous storm gathering in far-off Egypt. The Soldan summons his hordes:

> Awake, ye men of Memphis! hear the clang
> Of Scythian trumpets; hear the basilisks,
> That, roaring, shake Damascus' turrets down!

The third scene shows Egypt and Arabia on the march, apparently irresistible, confident of victory:

> Now, Tamburlaine, the mighty Soldan comes,
> And leads with him the great Arabian king,
> To dim thy baseness and obscurity!

And while the storm clouds gather, Tamburlaine, careless of the future, vaunts himself in the height of tragic *hybris*. He joys in the humiliations of the captive Bajazet and Zabina, blind to their sufferings, reckless of their curses and prayers for vengeance. The whole act is, as a fourth act should be, a breathless triumph of suspense; and in the last lines the hero makes a yet more wanton demand of fortune:

> We mean to travel to th' antarctic pole,
> Conquering the people underneath our feet,
> And be renowned as never emperors were.
> Zenocrate, I will not crown thee yet,
> Until with greater honors I be graced.

Whom the gods wish to ruin, they first make mad. The Soldan and Arabia, we know, are thundering against him. Will this mad, adorable romanticist ever survive their shock?

In the fifth act, the clouds darken, suspense thickens. "Still doth this man, or rather god of war batter" at the walls of Damascus, regardless of the brewing storm. The virgins move him not. By their slaughter he vindicates his Elizabethan consistency and throws another gauntlet into the teeth of Nemesis. Then lest tragic pity be lost to sight in all this accumulation of tragic terror, the stage is voided, and the man of war exposes in one of the grandest of all soliloquies the heart of the lover, the soul of the idealist:

> Ah, fair Zenocrate! divine Zenocrate!
>
> . . . . .
>
> What is beauty, saith my sufferings, then?
> If all the pens that ever poets held
> Had fed the feeling of their masters' thoughts,
> And every sweetness that inspir'd their hearts,
> Their minds, and muses on admired themes;
> If all the heavenly quintessence they still [distil]
> From their immortal flowers of poesy,
> Wherein, as in a mirror, we perceive
> The highest reaches of a human wit—
> If these had made *one* poem's period,
> And all combin'd in beauty's worthiness,
> Yet should there hover in their restless heads,
> *One* thought, *one* grace, *one* wonder at the least,
> Which into words no virtue can digest?

There follow the deaths of Bajazet and Zabina, another heavy weight added to the scale of Nemesis. Does not the fate of Tamburlaine now totter perceptibly in the balance? So Zenocrate thinks, as she wrestles in prayer for the life of her lover:

> Ah Tamburlaine, my love, sweet Tamburlaine,
> That fight'st for sceptres and for slippery crowns,
> Behold the Turk and his great emperess!
> Thou that in conduct of thy happy stars,
> Sleep'st every night with conquest on thy brows,

> And yet wouldst shun the wavering turns of war . . .
> Behold the Turk and his great emperess!
> Ah mighty Jove and holy Mahomet,
> Pardon my love! [10]

At this point, the blow, hanging during two acts in the air, falls at last. Enter Philemus to announce:

> Madam, your father and the Arabian king . . . come now,
> Ready for battle gainst my lord the king.

If all this is not dramatic, what is drama? Who can possibly presage the result? We can but wait, heart in mouth. But drama having had its say, romance may claim a hearing. "They sound to the battle within; and Tamburlaine enjoys the victory." And so after two idyllic pages of reconciliation, the tragedy closes on the Greek note: pity and terror, followed by serenity and beauty infinite. What better prologue than a play like this to an age of glorious tragedy?

So much for the least mature of Marlowe's greater plays. Much he learned from later practice concerning the mechanics of stage presentation,[11] but he was indeed a dramatist born.[12]

LAYING aside the gratuitous imaginings of modern fiction and the untruthful slaver of the contemporary enemies of his art, let us for a moment consider those qualities of Marlowe's personality which are most clearly mirrored in his writings.

10. Lines 2137 ff.

11. Note, for example, the great increase in animation of dialogue. The first part of *Tamburlaine*, containing 2308 dramatic lines, has 391 speeches; *Edward II*, with 2670 lines, has 952 speeches.

12. I omit here a section on Marlowe's death and the contemporary rumors about it. Its value has been destroyed by the discoveries of Professors Hotson and Eccles. For Professor Brooke's final word on Marlowe's life and death see his *Life of Marlowe and the Tragedy of Dido* (1930). Ed.

First, then, he was, like Spenser, a scholar—one of the truest of his time. Obviously, he loved learning deeply and hated pedantry. Few English poets—perhaps none but Spenser and Milton—have so splendidly vindicated the literary uses of sound learning. Marlowe is never more the poet than when he is most the scholar: in the address to Helen in *Faustus* or in Tamburlaine's comparison of Zenocrate to the heroines of classic literature:

> Had she lived before the siege of Troy,
> Helen, whose beauty summoned Greece to arms,
> And drew a thousand ships to Tenedos,
> Had not been named in Homer's Iliads,—
> Her name had been in every line he wrote;
> Or had those wanton poets, for whose birth
> Old Rome was proud, but gazed a while on her,
> Nor Lesbia nor Corinna had been named,—
> Zenocrate had been the argument
> Of every epigram or elegy: [13]

in Æneas' story of the wooden horse:

> Then he [Sinon] unlocked the horse, and suddenly,
> From out his entrails, Neoptolemus,
> Setting his spear upon the ground, leapt forth,
> And after him a thousand Grecians more,
> In whose stern faces shined the quenchless fire,
> That after burnt the pride of Asia: [14]

or finally, in the numberless passages which give immortal value to the sixteenth-century accomplishment in geography, astronomy, and philosophy. Marlowe's scholarship gave him his marvelous sense of form—form in the single line, in the scene, in the play as a whole—and the sense of form was precisely the rarest and most necessary of all virtues in Elizabethan poetry. Marlowe's scholarship gave

13. *II Tamburlaine*, ll. 3054 ff.
14. *Dido*, ll. 477 ff.

him the scholar's passion for truth—for fair play in intellectual disputes. In an age of unusual bigotry and self-assertion, his is almost the only voice raised in defense of alien races and alien creeds. Even the unspeakable Turk and the un-Christian Jew are justified by the sincerity of their faith.

And finally, the poet's scholarship gives him one of his most splendid virtues in his fiery hatred of hypocrisy. The religious atmosphere of Elizabeth's reign was full of sophistication and deceit. Against this Marlowe cries out with a voice more daring and more eloquent than that of even Spenser. Better a true Turk or a consistent Jew than a faithless and timeserving Christian. What more blasting exposure of the essential unchristianity of Christian politics than that which Marlowe puts into the mouth of the Turk Orcanes:

> Can there be such deceit in Christians,
> Or treason in the fleshly heart of man,
> Whose shape is figure of the highest God?
> Then, if there be a Christ, as Christians say,
> But in their deeds deny him for their Christ,
> If he be son to everliving Jove,
> And hath the power of his outstretched arm,
> If he be jealous of his name and honour,
> As is our holy prophet Mahomet . . .
> If there be Christ, we shall have victory.[15]

And what more splendid vindication of the cardinal principle of all religion, and of the practical truth that honesty is the best policy—even in diplomacy—than the ensuing overthrow and death of the treacherous Sigismund?

Not different is the moral drawn from the relations between the Christians and the Jews. After the hateful cant with which the Governor of Malta covers his iniquitous pillage of the Hebrews:

15. *II Tamburlaine*, ll. 2893 ff.

Through our sufferance of your hateful lives,
Who stand accursed in the sight of heaven,
These taxes and afflictions are befallen,[16]

(and therefore the tribute money of the Turks shall all
be levied among the Jews)—after this exposition of the
Christian spirit, is it surprising that Barabas indignantly
declines baptism, or that he later turns the Christian argument with invincible logic against themselves?

It's no sin to deceive a Christian;
For they themselves hold it a principle,
Faith is not to be held with heretics:
But all are heretics that are not Jews?[17]

One needs but little acquaintance with the history of
religious controversy to understand why the prelatists
and the Puritans alike flinched before this reasoning and
sought to drown the logic of the poet with cries of "libertine" and "atheist." "Let the galled jade wince." Silly such
clamor must have appeared even to contemporaries in view
of the tremendous close of Tamburlaine and the whole
mighty lesson of *Faustus;* in view of the deep earnestness
of every word Marlowe wrote.

So MUCH for Marlowe's intellectual character. His personal character reveals itself no less vividly. In the first
place, he held himself high, and though plying a vulgar
trade, refused to be vulgarized. Not even from his Puritan
defamers do we hear concerning him stories of low associations such as cling to the memory of Greene and Peele.
Except for Nashe's slight connection with *Dido,* he admitted no man to partnership in his literary enterprises.
Perhaps he needed money, but there is no record that he
ever descended to the acceptance of loans or familiarities

16. *Jew of Malta,* ll. 295 ff.
17. *Ibid.,* ll. 1074 ff.

from such men as Henslowe, who patronized and pauperized most of the dramatists of the day.

In this matter Marlowe and Shakespeare stand almost alone. To his familiars he was Kit Marlowe. Such were his fellow scholar, Nashe; the grave and learned Chapman, and Sir Walter Ralegh himself. The company of his friends seems to have been as small, however, as it was select; [18] and with all Europe he stood, like Falstaff, upon his dignity. The printer of *Tamburlaine*, dedicating the two plays to the Gentlemen-Readers in 1590, allows himself none of the usual liberties. He is but a tradesman presenting one gentleman to others. "Great folly were it in me," he writes, "to commend unto your wisdoms either the eloquence of the author . . . or the worthiness of the matter itself."

Thomas Heywood, introducing the 1633 edition of the *Jew of Malta*, refers ceremoniously to the author (then dead forty years) as "Mr. Marlo"; and the most gentlemanly of the publishers of the time, Edward Blount, writes a dedication of *Hero and Leander* to Sir Thomas Walsingham, the language of which, considering the exalted dignity of the person addressed, would of itself disprove the idea that Marlowe could have been accused by those who knew him of low associations.

"Sir," Blount writes, "we think not ourselves discharged of the duty we owe to our friend, when we have brought the breathless body to the earth: for albeit the eye there taketh his ever farewell of that beloved object, yet the impression of the man that hath been dear unto us, living an after life in our memory, there putteth us in mind of farther obsequies due unto the deceased . . . I suppose

18. Kyd, in his defamatory letter to Puckering, mentions as special friends of Marlowe, "Harriot, Warner, Royden, and some stationers [book-publishers] in Paul's Churchyard." There was nothing disreputable about any of these.

myself executor to the unhappily deceased author of this poem, upon whom knowing that in his lifetime you bestowed many kind favors, entertaining the parts of reckoning and worth which you found in him with good countenance and liberal affection: I cannot but see so far into the will of him dead, that whatsoever issue of his brain should chance to come abroad, that (he should wish) that the first breath it should take might be the gentle air of your liking: for since his self had been accustomed thereunto, it would prove more agreeable and thriving to his right children than any other foster countenance whatsoever. . . . Of a double duty, the one to yourself, the other to the deceased, I present the same to your most favorable allowance."

This was written five years after Marlowe's death, and Puritan tongues were already wagging. In the circumstances, it is certainly not the language a cautious and reputable publisher would use in coupling one of the noblest names in England with the name of a dead atheist and profligate. Let me conclude, therefore, by considering the particular topic which this dedication and the poem it introduces, *Hero and Leander*, naturally suggest: the moral side of the poet's character.

"Slain by a bawdy serving man, a rival of his in his lewd love." So wrote the puritanical Francis Meres in this same year 1598, basing his statement confessedly upon that of a yet more outrageous Puritan pamphleteer, Thomas Beard, who based his upon hearsay.[19] Well, it might be true. If it were, we need abate our admiration of Marlowe's genius not at all; our respect for his character, considering the manners of his age, not perhaps a great deal. But is it true? Hardly, I think. Read *Hero and Leander*. The subject of this poem is one of the most beautifully sensuous stories

19. Meres, however, is the only early writer who accuses Marlowe of sensuality.

in all the pagan literature of Greece, and the treatment
Marlowe gives it is one of the most translucently pure
things in sixteenth-century literature. What an opportunity for the sensual mind! In what Marlowe wrote there is
not an obscene word or a degenerate suggestion. Everywhere we have simply the marriage of true minds; the
perfect purity of ocean-dewy limbs and naked childlike
souls.

Alas, it is not always so in Elizabethan poetry. Compare
the two poems of Shakespeare; compare, indeed, any of
the many other treatments of such themes. Even in the
verse of *Hero and Leander* there seems to me a charming
reticence. In Marlowe's couplets there is no fluent and suggestive ease; there is, on the contrary, a sweet hesitancy,
not otherwise characteristic of the poet, which almost suggests diffidence, which cools instead of inflaming the
mind. And everywhere there is perfect moral poise; everywhere there are grave and wise and tender observations
as of a soul firm-fastened in its roots:

> Where both deliberate, the love is slight;
> Who ever loved that loved not at first sight?
>
> Love is not full of pity, as men say,
> But deaf and cruel where he means to prey.
>
> Faithful love will never turn to hate.
>
> It lies not in our power to love or hate,
> For will in us is overruled by fate.

Am I making too much of this? Does it greatly matter
today whether a poet who died in 1593 lived his life like
Byron or like Keats? I think it matters still, but the question is one of fact. Marlowe's entire original work [20] seems
to me to prove that something of the abhorrence of im-
pure suggestion which experience of life taught the great

20. I hold no brief for the immature Ovid translation.

Shakespeare to express in Desdemona, in Imogen, and in Miranda, was innate in Marlowe and remained with him to the end. How else can we explain the fervor with which he vindicates the chastity of his remorseless Scythian conqueror; how else the refusal in the case of the great sensualist Faustus to dwell upon any sensual suggestion, and the splendid purity that makes the lines to Helen a veritable hymn? [21] How else can we explain the tender treatment of Abigail and the yet tenderer effort to extenuate the open sin of Isabella?

Verily, the wicked have digged a pit and have fallen into it themselves. Puritanism has unmasked itself. Let us believe, if you like, with the informant, Richard Baines, that Marlowe intended to counterfeit the currency of the realm. There is nothing in the poet's works to disprove that. But to imagine the author of *Faustus* an atheist, the author of *Hero and Leander* a sensualist—that were an ignominy and shame indeed!

21. Note also the pure loveliness, which naturally attracted Walton, in the song of "The Passionate Shepherd."

ON READING SPENSER

WHO is the greatest of the Elizabethan poets? To such a question Ben Jonson's cohorts would have shouted truculently "Rare Ben!" into the ears of all and sundry; but in his truly rarest mood Ben himself, I am sure, would have winked a roguish eye, sworn his auditors to secrecy, and whispered, "Will Shakespeare." Shakespeare, loyal dramatist that he was, would have voted for Kit Marlowe; and Marlowe, without a pause or a pang, would have transferred the laurel to his master, Spenser.

The last would have been beyond all comparison the most popular Elizabethan choice; in it unites, indeed, a well-nigh universal chorus of the poet's contemporaries, from Robert Allott, who in his anthology, *England's Parnassus* (1600), can content himself with no fewer than 387 Spenserian extracts, to all the motley but unanimous critics who saw in Spenser the only modern equal to the greatest of the ancients. "The only living Homer," "our Homer," "Edmund Spenser, Homerus Britannicus"; so with no dissenting voice runs the verdict of the age.

And the Elizabethan answer is in sooth the only reply, for Shakespeare is not of an age but for all time. The bard of Avon, most successful perhaps of all the poets of the world, owed much of his success to his care in rendering unto Caesar the things that are Caesar's and laying up his finest treasures for generations yet unborn. From his own age Shakespeare asked and obtained a fellow-ship in a cry of players, with the solid emoluments thereto appertaining. He obtained his ease at the Boarshead, Mermaid, and the gentle hostelries along the Stratford road. He acquired the arms and title of a gentleman, and ultimately broad

meadow lands in Warwickshire, with the spacious leisure
of New Place.

Willingly he relinquished the regal immortality of
Westminster, by the side of Chaucer and Spenser and Ben
Jonson, for undisturbed repose in the chancel of his provincial church. Once in early life Shakespeare vouchsafed
a scant dozen lines of compliment to the Virgin Queen;
twice, likewise at the opening of his career, he deigned to
dedicate a poem to a noble patron. This is almost the whole
extent of Shakespeare's concession to his age. The characters of his plays he selected with curious perversity from
Veronese and Frenchmen, Venetians, Romans, Germans,
Jews, Danes, Moors, and ancient Britons—from every
nationality but the subjects of his queen. Of the English
of the past he is an unrivaled delineator; of the Englishmen of his own time he hardly tells us directly anything except that they dress outlandishly, outdrink the
Dutch, and are stupidly given to staring at strange monsters.

It was to gentle Master Spenser that Englishmen turned
during the great years between 1579 and 1599, and have
turned ever since, for the clearest-souled and clearest-eyed
interpretation of the greatest English age: to Spenser, who
first restored Chaucer to his primacy among English poets
and first gave him a companion, a rival, and a noble expositor, who first after Chaucer raised poetry from the
casual pastime of idle hours and made it again the inspiration, the guide, and consecration of mankind; and who first
of all Englishmen really combined the powers of the
singer and the prophet.

London-born, Cambridge-bred, an ardent and gracious
courtier, the friend of all the noblest spirits of the time,
the knight-errant of righteousness, the gallant adventurer
in realms beyond the sea, the constant foe of social or
political corruption and all unmanliness, the arch embodi-

ment of the infinite wonder and splendor of life well lived:
Spenser was in the eyes of his contemporaries incompa-
rably the greatest English man of letters—the most potent
force in English literature.

Much is said foolishly of the unfairness of contemporary
judgments of poetry. I cannot find that, in English literature at least, a first-class writer has ever lacked during his
lifetime first-class appreciation. Belial and all his sons could
not prevent *Paradise Lost* from becoming the greatest literary success of the Restoration age and Milton admittedly
its greatest poet. Shakespeare, Marlowe, and Ben Jonson,
though they made themselves a motley to the view and
catered to what the prejudice of the time was prone to
account a mechanical trade rather than an art, attained a
height of contemporary reputation doubtless far beyond
their most sanguine hopes, and created an entirely new
position for dramatic literature.

The stories of great poets deceased in penury—Chaucer, Spenser, Dryden—must be added to the long list of
fabrications in which human mediocrity appears to find a
solace. They may be classed with the pleasant fictions
which teach that poets never understand practical affairs
and that great artists are always long-haired eccentrics.
But let that pass. Why read Spenser today? Let us put the
question and stay for several answers.

FIRST—and this should be regarded as no paradox—because *The Fairy Queen* is for variety of character and incident, magnificent skill of structure—yea, and for com-
pression—one of the marvels of the world's fiction. Rest
the soul of Macaulay! Far be it from me to draw unnecessary attention to the slips of one whom none but the
mustiest pedant can read without profit and delight. This,
however, is part of what he wrote in an evil hour when

he had allowed the dust to grow thick upon his Spenser.[1]
Nay, even Spenser himself, though assuredly one of the
greatest poets that ever lived, could not succeed in the
attempt to make allegory interesting. One unpardonable
fault, the fault of tediousness, pervades the whole of *The
Fairy Queen*."

Allegory, forsooth! If *The Fairy Queen* is allegorical,
so are *Hamlet* and *Vanity Fair* and *The Book of Job*. It
was no mystic fantasy that one of the keenest patriots,
colonists, and politicians of his age read to Walter Ralegh
and dedicated to "Elizabeth, by the grace of God Queen
of England, France, and Ireland and of Virginia . . . to
live with the eternity of her fame." It was not allegorical
symbolism of any ordinary kind which he introduced by
fourteen dedicatory sonnets to the greatest lords of the
nation—for which the penurious queen is reported to
have ordered the poet the then huge pension of £50 per
annum, and for which the yet more penurious Burghley
did actually pay him the annual equivalent of at least
$2,000 a year.

Tedious, indeed! The entire extant *corpus* of *The Fairy
Queen*, including the various prefatory stanzas, amounts
to about 280,000 words. Thackeray's *Vanity Fair* contains
340,000; and *Vanity Fair* is not an unduly long novel, as
the greater pieces of English fiction go. Spenser uses as
much language as DeMorgan or Arnold Bennett would
employ in tracing the love affair of a couple of human
mediocrities or Richardson would squander upon a single
genteel flirtation. And what unparalleled effects he does
accomplish!

Here we have in truth the ideal novel, the picture of

1. It should be remembered, of course, that Macaulay's unfortunate
passage on Spenser is a mere *obiter dictum*, dashed off rashly when his
mind was full of Bunyan.

life as it is, without a hero or a heroine. In three of the
books, indeed—the first, second, and fifth—the doings of
the particular knight celebrated occupy a major part of
the contents; but in each of these books a different knight
is treated, while in the other three a central figure hardly
exists. Spenser's Fairyland is the true democracy of life.
The poet plays no favorites among his characters, uses no
pedestals and no foreshortenings. Hardly elsewhere, I suppose, has a poet's imagination succeeded in portraying the
real course of human affairs with such perfect art and so
little of the claptrap of structural artifice. Spenser's men
and women pursue their careers through ever fresh and
apparently unpremeditated incidents, resisting or yielding
to the natural temptations they encounter, performing
their heroisms and their meannesses, resting in wayside
cottages or castles, or under the shade of trees; lost sometimes for long series of cantos to the reader but always
reappearing in the natural progress of events; never hurried on to forced conclusions; always advancing from task
to task in the simple human way.

While life lasts, interest continues and duty drives. The
Red Cross Knight accomplishes early his great devoir. He
slays the dragon and wins his lady; but wedding bells do
not sweep him off the stage and leave the rest to silence.
The later books see him again and again, following his
godly course, bearing modestly his laurels, aiding his
friends, resisting his foes, doing his duty as an English
gentleman should do, and losing no scintilla of his interest
because he no longer occupies the center of the stage.
Spenser has no minor characters: they are all principals,
all the size of life.

None of the Elizabethan poets is less dramatic in the
ordinary sense than Spenser. None, however, but Shakespeare can approach him in the fundamental business of
the dramatist: the impartial presentation of different types

of character. Of all the English poets, indeed, it may be said that none but Shakespeare and Chaucer can compare with Spenser in his magnificent ability to keep his hands off his figures, to let each play his own part with all the independence of nature.

And for this, forsooth, they call *The Fairy Queen* tedious; they say it lacks coherence and structure and definiteness of plot!

The third book is a good example of the poet's method. It is entitled the Book of Chastity, and concerns itself, in fact, almost wholly with the aspect of life involved in the treatment of that virtue and its opposite. The first three cantos and the last two deal chiefly with the exploits of Britomart, the titular heroine of the book; but in none of the intermediate seven cantos is she the main figure. Thus the beautiful legend of Britomart is thrown round the book like the hoops about a bulging cask. But Britomart is for Spenser much more than a symbol of chastity, and her destiny carries her far beyond the limits of the book to which she gives her name.

So Chastity, "That fairest virtue, far above the rest," is infinitely too manifold in its human variations to be made the particular embellishment of a single individual. It reveals itself in the third book in many types of women: in the knightly maiden Britomart, seeking with passionate longing the just Sir Artegall, long since revealed to her in the magic mirror as her destined husband. It shows itself otherwise in the huntress Belphoebe, vowed to Diana and immune from human passion, yet softly human in her tender ministrations to the wounded squire; human also in the pique she feels when Timias shows a momentary touch of sentiment for another maid. Again Chastity is glorified in the virgin wife Amoret, kidnapped on her wedding day but triumphantly resisting through long months the superhuman torments and temptations of her captor. And once more the virtue appears in the radiant Florimel, the charming lady of the court, whose pretty story shoots like a gold thread through all the rainbow colors of the third, fourth, and fifth books, as she braves the terrors of forest and of sea to save her reluctant lover Marinel.

Here, surely, is "God's plenty"; and here in the midst of Gloriana's Fairyland is unfolded the true picture of our world, as each character confronts her own joys and sorrows, unafraid and in general unassisted.

Let it not be supposed that Spenser's characters enjoy in Fairyland any exemption from the evils of actual life. With all its lovely virtue, there is nothing saccharine about the book. The woods are full of loathly foresters, the sea has its lewd fishermen, and knightly armor sometimes hides the poltroon and deceiver. In two cantos of Book III, Spenser, with quite Italianesque realism, sets off his pictures of chastity by the unchaste story of the gay Lothario, Sir Paridell, the jealous Malbecco, and the wanton Hellenore. They fill in the sketch of life, and the greatness of the book shows in this, that Paridell and Hellenore seem as genuinely native to the story, as thoroughly entitled to their existence, as Britomart herself.

So then the poem moves, one of the truest human comedies ever essayed by artist, and vastly the most beautiful. Still beginning, never ending, character is added to character, incident to incident, and our motley human life flows on past the windows of Kilcolman Castle, where sits the poet, glorying in the noble, looking evil square in the face, but keeping his hands off. Here, if ever, is art concealing art. Every stanza, every canto, every episode grows to its perfection as inevitably and inconspicuously as if the sun and rain of heaven fostered it. Here is the apotheosis of method, the *ne plus ultra* of structure. In the face of this, one may at times be tempted even to blaspheme against the great gods of Olympus. Even Chaucer's art may look puerile, as he breaks his bundle of sticks one by one, carefully dropping one character, finishing one story, before he ventures upon the next. And beside the tidal flow of Spenser even the great dramatist's method, with its gross catastrophes, spotlights, its overhaste and bluster, may sometimes seem like tinsel against moonlight.

Of course, Spenser has his conventions, as needs the artist must; but they are conventions which enlarge instead of cramping, freshen instead of jading. Fairyland is one. "The world is too much with us." He multiplies it by infinity, and gives it a new, universal charm. His characters are Fairies, Britons, Moslems, Dwarfs, Enchanters, Savage Men—all the masks the heart of man can wear; but the masks never conceal the real men and women; they impress us always as beautiful externals, as so many gorgeous and exquisitely fitting costumes of the human soul. And various as are the masks, they cannot equal in diversity Spenser's types of humanity.[2]

WHY read Spenser? Indeed reasons are as plentiful as blackberries. Because to his uncanny skill in narrative he adds a power of description quite unsurpassed in English poetry. The paths of Fairyland are the main-traveled roads of Elizabethan Ireland; they are the perennial thoroughfares of human nature. Here is an Irish cottage, seen at nightfall, with its occupants. Has Synge anywhere done it better?

> So long she traveild, till at length she came
> To an hilles side, which did to her bewray
> A little valley subject to the same
> All coverd with thick woodes that quite it overcame.
> Through th' tops of the high trees she did descry
> A little smoke, whose vapour thin and light

2. Another convention is the knightly quest.

Reeking aloft uprolled to the sky:
Which chearefull signe did send unto her sight
That in the same did wonne some living wight.
Eftsoones her steps she thereunto applyd,
And came at last in weary wretched plight
Unto the place, to which her hope did guyde
To finde some refuge there, and rest her wearie syde.

There in a gloomy hollow glen she found
A little cottage, built of stickes and reedes
In homely wize, and wald with sods around;
In which a witch did dwell, in loathly weedes
And wilfull want, all carelesse of her needes;
So choosing solitarie to abide
Far from all neighbours, that her divelish deedes
And hellish arts from people she might hide,
And hurt far off unknowne whomever she envide.

This wicked woman had a wicked sonne,
The comfort of her age and weary dayes,
A laesy loord, for nothing good to donne,
But stretched forth in ydlenesse alwayes,
Ne ever cast his mind to covet prayse,
Or ply himselfe to any honest trade;
But all the day before the sunny rayes
He us'd to slug, or sleepe in slothfull shade
Such laesienesse both lewd and poor attonce him made.[3]

Here is Irish rustic hospitality:

But Melibee (so hight that good old man)
Now seeing Calidore left all alone,
And night arrived hard at hand, began
Him to invite unto his simple home;
Which though it were a cottage clad with lome,
And all things therein meane, yet better so
To lodge then in the salvage fields to rome.

3. Bk. III. vii, 4–6, 12.

The knight full gladly soone agreed thereto,
Being his harts owne wish; and home with him did go.

There he was welcom'd of that honest syre
And of his aged beldame homely well;
Who him besought himselfe to disattyre,
And rest himselfe, till supper time befell;
By which home came the fayrest Pastorell,
After her flocke she in their fold had tyde;
And, supper readie dight, they to it fell
With small adoe, and nature satisfyde,
The which doth litle crave contented to abyde.[4]

Here is the Irish deserted village better almost than even
Goldsmith could paint it:

Who when he backe returned from the wood,
And saw his shepheards cottage spoyled quight,
And his love reft away; he wexed wood
And halfe enraged at that ruefull sight;
That even his heart, for very fell despight,
And his owne flesh he readie was to teare:
He chauft, he griev'd, he fretted, and he sigh't,
And fared like a furious wyld beare,
Whose whelpes are stolne away, she being otherwhere.

Ne wight he found to whom he might complaine,
Ne wight he found of whom he might inquire;
That more increast the anguish of his paine:
He sought the woods, but no man could see there;
He sought the plaines, but could no tidings heare:
The woods did nought but ecchoes vaine rebound;
The playnes all waste and emptie did appeare;
Where wont the shepheards oft their pypes resound,
And feed an hundred flocks, there now not one be found.

At last, as there he romed up and downe,
He chaunst one coming towards him to spy,

4. Bk. VI. ix, 16, 17.

> That seem'd to be some sorie simple clowne,
> With ragged weedes, and lockes upstaring hye,
> As if he did from some late daunger fly,
> And yet his feare did follow him behynd:
> Who as he unto him approached nye,
> He mote perceive, by signes which he did fynd,
> That Coridon it was, the silly shepheards hynd.[5]

Here are the scavenger hounds by the Irish roadside:

> Like as a sort of hungry dogs, ymet
> About some carcase by the common way,
> Doe fall together, stryving each to get
> The greatest portion of the greedie pray;
> All on confused heapes themselves assay,
> And snatch, and byte, and rend, and tug, and teare;
> That who them sees would wonder at their fray,
> And who sees not would be affrayd to heare. . . .[6]

Here are a couple of vivid hunting scenes:

> Like as a fearefull partridge, that is fledd
> From the sharpe hauke which her attached neare,
> And fals to ground to seeke for succor theare,
> Whereas the hungry spaniells she does spye
> With greedy iawes her ready for to teare:
> In such distresse and sad perplexity
> Was Florimell, when Proteus she did see her by.[7]

> As salvage bull, whom two fierce mastives bayt,
> When rancour doth with rage him once engorge,
> Forgets with warywarde them to awayt,
> But with his dreadfull hornes them drives afore,
> Or flings aloft, or treades downe in the flore,
> Breathing out wrath, and bellowing disdaine,
> That all the forest quakes to hear him rore. . . .[8]

5. Bk. VI, xi, 25–27.
6. Bk. VI, xi, 17.
7. Bk. III, viii, 33.
8. Bk. II, viii, 42.

Here is the last scene viewed from the dog's point of view:

> Like as a mastiffe having at a bay
> A salvage bull, whose cruell hornes doe threat
> Desperate daunger if he them assay,
> Traceth his ground, and round about doth beat,
> To spy where he may some advantage get,
> The whiles the beast doth rage and loudly rore. . . .[9]

And here, finally, are the small things of nature, the gnats and flies and little birds, in which Spenser always felt a special interest:

> For as a bittur in the eagles clawe,
> That may not hope by flight to scape alive,
> Still waytes for death with dread and trembling aw;
> So he, now subject to the victours law,
> Did not once move, nor upward cast his eye.[10]

> Like as a goshauke, that in foote doth beare
> A trembling culver, having spide on hight
> An eagle that with plumy wings doth sheare
> The subtile ayre stouping with all his might,
> The quarrey throwes to ground with fell despight,
> And to the batteill doth herselfe prepare. . . .[11]

> As when a swarme of gnats at eventide
> Out of the fennes of Allan doe arise
> Their murmuring small trompetts sownden wide,
> Whiles in the aire their clustring army flies,
> That as a cloud doth seeme to dim the skies;
> Ne man nor beast may rest or take repast
> For their sharpe wounds and noyous iniuries,
> Till the fierce northerne wind with blustring blast
> Doth blow them quite away, and in the ocean cast.[12]

9. Bk. VI, vii, 47.
10. Bk. II, viii, 50.
11. Bk. III, vii, 39.
12. Bk. II, ix, 16.

> How many flyes in whottest summers day
> Do seize upon some beast, whose flesh is bare,
> That all the place with swarmes do overlay,
> And with their little stings right felly fare;
> So many theeves about him swarming are,
> All which do him assayle on every side.[13]

Surely it is no vague and vacuous Fairyland which shows two or three such pictures on every page.

WHY read Spenser? Because, so long as this world remains a scene of strife; so long as high ideals must combat with low, and the Christian Knights of Maidenhead continue to level spear against the Paynim host, against the wiles of Busirane and the entrenched might of Grantorto, *The Fairy Queen* will remain a chief guide, incentive, and consoler. It is no lotus land that Spenser creates. No other poet has painted with more terrible truth the images of Despair, Slander, Care, Envy and Detraction, the Blatant Beast of Scandal, and the brazen Dragon of Sin. These are academic abstractions to nobody who has ever come to grips with life. To Spenser and the great men of his age, to all the noble spirits to whom since *The Fairy Queen* has been an inspiration next only to the Bible and to Shakespeare, these things have appeared among the most real and significant forces in the world.

If the monsters seem to us less near or menacing—if indeed!—let us give thanks and be trebly watchful. But it will be a long age before the adventurer on our earth will cease to meet them and a yet longer mayhap ere he finds elsewhere armor as adequate and imperishable as that which Spenser offers. Here are the weapons by which Spenser's knights conquer:

13. Bk. VI, xi, 48.

1. Generosity

O! Goodly golden chayne, wherewith yfere
The vertues linked are in lovely wize;
And noble mindes of yone allyed were,
In brave poursuitt of chevalrous emprize,
That none did others safety despize,
Nor did envy to him, in need that stands;
But friendly each did others praise devize,
How to advaunce with favourable hands,
As this good prince redeemd the Redcrosse knight from
     bands.[14]

2. Simple truth

But antique age, yet in the infancie
Of time, did live then, like an innocent,
In simple truth and blameless chastitie;
Ne then of guile had made experiment;
But, voide of vile and treacherous intent,
Held vertue, for itselfe, in soveraine awe:
Then loyal love had royall regiment,
And each unto his lust did make a lawe,
From all forbidden things his liking to withdraw.[15]

3. Aid to the weak

Nought is more honourable to a knight,
No better doth beseeme brave chevalry,
Then to defend the feeble in their right,
And wrong redresse in such as wend awry:
Whilome those great heroes got thereby
Their greatest glory for their rightfull deedes,
And place deserved with the gods on hy:
Herein the noblesse of this knight exceedes,
Who now to perils great for iustice sake proceedes.[16]

14. Bk. I, ix, 1.
15. Bk. IV, viii, 30.
16. Bk. V, ii, 1.

4. The power of Justice

It often fals, in course of common life,
That right long time is overborne of wrong
Through avarice, or powre, or guile, or strife,
That weakens her, and makes her party strong:
But iustice, though her dome she doe prolong,
Yet at the last she will her owne cause right:
As by sad Belgè seemes; whose wrongs though long
She suffred, yet at length she did requight,
And sent redresse thereof by this brave Briton knight.[17]

5. Self-control

Was never man, who most conquéstes atchiev'd,
But sometimes had the worse, and lost by warre;
Yet shortly gaynd, that losse exceeded farre;
Losse is no shame, nor to bee lesse then foe;
But to bee lesser than himselfe doth marre
Both loosers lott, and victour's prayse alsóe:
Vaine others overthrowes who selfe doth overthrow.[18]

For nothing is more blamefull to a knight,
That court'sie doth as well as armes professe,
However strong and fortunate in fight,
Then the reproch of pride and cruelnesse:
In vaine he seeketh others to suppresse,
Who hath not learnd himselfe first to subdew:
All flesh is frayle and full of ficklenesse,
Subiect to fortunes chance, still chaunging new;
What haps to day to me to morrow may to you.[19]

6. Courtesy

> What vertue is so fitting for a knight,
> Or for a ladie whom a knight should love,
> As curtesie; to beare themselves aright

17. Bk. V, xi, 1.
18. Bk. V, ii, 15.
19. Bk. VI, i, 41.

To all of each degree as doth behove?
For whether they be placed high above
Or low beneath, yet ought they well to know
Their good: that none them rightly may reprove
Of rudenesse for not yeelding what they owe:
Great skill it is such duties timely to bestow.[20]

WHY read Spenser once more? Because he is the poets'
poet. How little we commonly understand the meaning
of the tribute! Of all men the poets are, I suppose, the
most practical and utilitarian in their reading of poetry.
The tired businessman and the aimless dilettante, the
lawyer, the grocer, and the drayman, may indeed look
upon poetry simply as a means of diversion. They perhaps
are often satisfied with mere sonorous lines—with "sound
and fury, signifying nothing." It takes vastly more than
that to hold the devotion of Marlowe and Milton, Dryden,
Pope, Coleridge, Wordsworth, Keats, and Shelley. These
are not men to stand agape before mere ease in riming or
languorous flow of idle narrative. They doff their caps
only to a master of thought, a great prophet and inspirer:
and such each of these has gratefully confessed in Spenser.

It was in no flight of poetical exaggeration, but in the
calm and measured prose of *Areopagitica*, that Milton
avowed his personal indebtedness to "our sage and serious
poet Spenser, whom I dare be known to think a better
teacher than Scotus or Aquinas." It was Spenser again
whom Milton thought of in *Il Penseroso* as the type and
pattern of all great bards:

And if aught else great bards beside
In sage and solemn tunes have sung,
Of tourneys and of trophies hung,
Of forests and enchantments drear,
Where more is meant than meets the ear.

20. Bk. VI, ii, 1.

Without the Bower of Acrasia, *Comus* would never have appeared in the form we know; without the *Shepherd's Calender*, *Lycidas* as we know it could hardly have been written. Without the inspiration and challenge of *The Fairy Queen*, it is perhaps doubtful whether *Paradise Lost* would ever have been conceived. Certainly, it would have lacked a hundred of its most glorious passages, if Spenser's stanzas had not reverberated for years in Milton's mind.

It was not for nought that Dryden coupled Milton's name with that of "his master Spenser, the author of that immortal poem called *The Fairy Queen*." "Milton," he says again (Preface to the *Fables*), "was the poetical son of Spenser." And Dryden's own sonship he was ever proud to own. "I must acknowledge," he says, "that Vergil in Latin and Spenser in English have been my masters."

"No man," he asserts elsewhere, "was ever born with a greater genius" than Spenser, "or had more knowledge to support it." Spenser he would place, "had his action been finished," beside Homer, Vergil, and Tasso as one of the four supreme epic poets of the world; as a pastoral poet he ranks him not inferior to the two great models in this style, Theocritus and Vergil.

The Hind and the Panther admits its obvious debt to "Mother Hubberd in her homely dress"; and Dryden, furthermore, was one of the many who, despite Macaulay's dictum, have passed the Blatant Beast and read on in *The Fairy Queen* unwearied. In the last of all the cantos (VII, vii) he found a definite inspiration and marked one of the stanzas in his copy of the poem as a "Groundwork for a Song on St. Cecilia's Day," Certainly, in the Spenser whom Milton and Dryden thus venerated there was little of the idle versifier, the gentle spinner of gossamer allegory.

Pope's first important work, the *Pastorals*, is confessedly an imitation of Spenser. "Looking upon Spenser as the father of the English pastoral," he says, "I thought myself unworthy to be esteemed even the meanest of his sons, unless I bore some resemblance of him . . . So I have copied Spenser in miniature and reduced his twelve months into four seasons." This he versifies as follows:

> That flute is mine, which Colin's tuneful mouth
> Inspir'd when living, and bequeath'd in death;
> He said: Alexis, take this pipe, the same
> That taught the grove my Rosalinda's name.

The Rape of the Lock is full of Spenserian reminiscences, and the noblest creation of Pope's genius, the perfect heroic couplet, was in truth but a recreation of what Spenser had accomplished in the same mode.

> Where shall we find in all our English verse,

asks Austin Dobson concerning Pope,

> A style more trenchant or a sense more terse?

Nowhere, is the answer, unless in Spenser. Here is a passage fit to set by the best of Pope—a passage at which one can safely wager that Pope's Spenser would have opened automatically:

> Full little knowest thou that hast not tried,
> What hell it is in suing long to bide:
> To lose good days, that might be better spent;
> To waste long nights in pensive discontent;
> To speed to-day, to be put back to-morrow;
> To feed on hope, to pine with fear and sorrow:
> To have thy Prince's grace, yet want her Peers';
> To have thy asking, yet wait many years;
> To fret thy soul with crosses and with cares;
> To eat thy heart through comfortless dispairs;
> To fawn, to crouch, to wait, to ride, to run,
> To spend, to give, to want, to be undone.[21]

21. *Mother Hubberd's Tale*, 895 ff.

And he who gave his finest weapon to the Wasp of Twickenham forged the celestial armor of Romance. It was in Spenser that the great Romantic movement found itself and gathered strength and triumphed. James Thomson in his *Seasons* and *Castle of Indolence* is of course Spenserian through and through. And it was in these significant words that Thomas Warton at the age of seventeen (1745) voiced his challenge to the Augustan poets:

> But let the sacred genius of the night
> Such mystic visions send as Spenser saw,
> When thro' bewild'ring Fancy's magic maze
> To the fell house of Busirane he led
> Th' unshaken Britomart . . .
> Thro' Pope's soft song though all the Graces breathe,
> And happiest art adorn his Attic page,
> Yet does my mind with sweeter transport glow,
> As at the foot of mossy trunk reclin'd,
> In magic Spenser's wildly-warbled song
> I see deserted Una wander wide
> Thro' wasteful solitudes, and lurid heaths,
> Weary, forlorn.

Later it was in his *Observations on the Fairy Queen of Spenser* (1754) that Warton carried the romantic controversy before the bar of criticism.

It was Spenser and ever Spenser—"Spenser gentlest bard divine" ("Monody on Death of Chatterton")—that Coleridge read with rapture during the wondrous days at Nether-Stowey. Spenser, as the critics have so often shown, inspired and shaped "The Ancient Mariner" and "Christabel." From one of his favorite characters in *The Fairy Queen*, Coleridge took the pseudonym with which he signed the *Satyrane-Letters*, written from Germany in 1799–1800. And when his admiration of the poetic gifts of Wordsworth could no farther go, he renounced his friend's baptismal name of William and solemnly rechristened him Edmund—and that though Shakespeare was a William! [22]

And Wordsworth! He can hardly write of what is most sacred and personal without a benediction on Spenser, the poet whom he had particularly studied in boyhood and whom he claimed at Cambridge as a brother:

> that gentle Bard,
> Chosen by the Muses for their page of state,—
> Sweet Spenser, moving through his clouded heaven
> With the moon's beauty and the moon's soft grace,
> I called him brother, Englishman, and friend.[23]

> The hemisphere
> Of magic fiction, verse of mine perchance
> May never tread; but scarcely Spenser's self
> Could have more tranquil visions in his youth,
> Or could more bright appearances create
> Of human forms with superhuman powers
> Than I beheld loitering on calm clear nights,
> Alone, beneath this fairy work of earth.[24]

It was thus that in dedicating the "White Doe of Rylstone" to his wife (1815) Wordsworth recalled one of the most poignant pleasures of their early married life:

> In trellised shade, with clustering roses gay,
> And, Mary, oft beside our blazing fire . . .
> Did we together read in Spenser's lay,
> How Una, sad of soul—in sad attire,
> The gentle Una, of celestial birth,
> To seek her knight went wandering o'er the earth.
> Ah, then, beloved! pleasing was the smart,
> And the tear precious in compassion shed
> For her, who pierced by sorrow's thrilling dart,

22. Cf. J. P. Collier, *Lectures on Sh. & Milton*, 32 f., 46 f., for talks of Coleridge and Wordsworth on Spenser.
23. *The Prelude*, III, 278 ff.
24. *Ibid.*, VI, 86 ff.

Did meekly bear the pang unmerited;
Meek as that emblem of her lowly heart,
The milk-white lamb which in a line she led,—
And faithful, loyal in her innocence,
Like the brave lion slain in her defence.

It was a chance reading of the *Epithalamion*, about 1812, that first turned the mind of the seventeen-year-old Keats to poetry. "As he listened," says Clarke, "his features and exclamations were ecstatic. . . . That night he took away with him a volume of the *Fairy Queen*, and he went through it as a young horse through a spring meadow, ramping."

"It was the *Fairy Queen*," repeats Brown, the friend of his later years, "that first awakened his genius. In Spenser's fairy land he was enchanted, breathed in a new world and became a new being; till enamoured of the stanza, he attempted to imitate it and succeeded."

"Nothing that is told of Orpheus or Amphion," says J. R. Lowell, "is more wonderful than this miracle of Spenser's, transforming a surgeon's apprentice into a great poet. Keats learned at once the secret of his birth."

Keats' first poem is thought to be his "Imitation of Spenser"; his first volume bore as its motto a couplet from *Muiopotmos*,

What more felicity can fall to creature
Than to enjoy delight with liberty?

Perhaps nothing that he thereafter wrote is wholly free from Spenserian allusion. "Endymion" is a perfect tissue of it. It was in "The Eve of St. Agnes," written in Spenser's stanza and under the strongest Spenserian influence, that Keats first achieved a complete success in the more ambitious type of poetry.

"The stanza," writes Professor de Sélincourt, "is not merely formally Spenserian; it is employed with a truly

Spenserian effect; and the subtle modulation of the melody, and in particular the lingering sweetness of the Alexandrine are nowhere else so effective outside *The Fairy Queen*. With the form Keats has at last perhaps caught something of that spirit of chivalry inherent in Spenser, which from the first he had desired to emulate. In his conception of Madeline Keats has realized the frame of mind which conceived of Una or Pastorella, and which inspired the *Epithalamion*, and is free at last from the mawkish sentimentality and misdirected sensuousness of his early love poetry."

By one of the most curious coincidences of poetic psychology, Keats likewise developed before his death the same superstitious feeling in regard to Spenser's Christian name which Coleridge and Wordsworth experienced—the same mystic fancy that a poet could not really flourish till he bore, like an old religious devotee, the name of his patron saint. In the last year of his life, he wrote to a friend cursing, only half in jest, his name of John, and adding, "If my name had been Edmund, I should have been more fortunate." And that though Milton's name was John.[25]

Keats has been called the truest Spenserian that ever lived, and his claim to the title would be hard to dispute; but there have been few English poets from Marlowe to Alfred Noyes of whom much the same might not be said. For three centuries Spenser has remained the surest touchstone of poetic values—in a very literal sense,

> The best and surest packet
> To the islands of the blest.

It is Keats' friend Leigh Hunt who in his sonnet on "The Dearest Poets" sums up better perhaps than anyone else Spenser's precise place among his peers:

25. Almost the last literary occupation of Keats, it is said, was to mark his favorite passages in a copy of Spenser destined for Fanny Brawne.

Were I to name, out of the times gone by,
The poets dearest to me, I should say,
Pulci for spirits, and a fine free way;
Chaucer for manners, and close silent eye;
Milton for classic taste, and harp strung high;
Spenser for luxury, and sweet, sylvan play;
Horace for chatting with, from day to day;
Shakespeare for all, but most, society.

But which take with me, could I take but one?
Shakespeare,—as long as I was unoppressed,
With the world's weight, making sad thoughts intenser;
But did I wish, out of the common sun
To lay a wounded heart in leafy rest,
And dream of things far off and healing,—Spenser.

Why read Spenser? Finally, because he is being read at this moment more generally and with more complete understanding than ever before. It is literally true that a student of Spenser today has to deal, so far as critical literature is concerned, with material decidedly more modern than that which engages the student of Tennyson. The real contributions to our knowledge of Tennyson during the present century cannot in any way compare with the new discoveries concerning Spenser. And the result is that what men of talent have always recognized intuitively is now known to every doctor of philosophy and is demonstrable to all.

Edmund Spenser can be alien to no intelligent reader of books; he must stand forever as one, and not the slightest, of the four great pillars that bear up the edifice of English literary civilization. The greatest of the true Elizabethans, friend of Sidney, Leicester, Ralegh, Essex; scholar, courtier, politician, colonist; most Puritan of poets, most poetical of Puritans: when we cease to read Spenser, may the Lord have mercy on our souls!